THE READER'S DIGEST

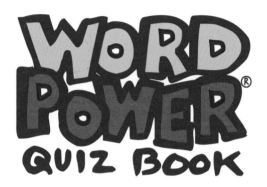

THE READER'S DIGEST

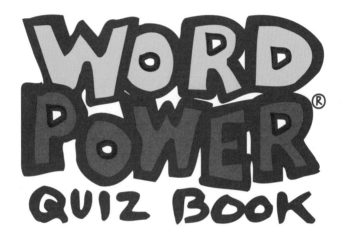

Over 1,000 word challenges from
America's most popular magazine

THE READER'S DIGEST ASSOCIATION, INC.
Pleasantville, New York/Montreal

Text design by Michele Italiano-Perla
Text illustration by Mike Quon Design

The credits that appear on page 224 are hereby made a part of this copyright page.
Copyright © 1995 by The Reader's Digest Association, Inc.
All rights reserved. Unauthorized reproduction, in any manner, is prohibited.

Library of Congress Cataloging in Publication Data
The Reader's Digest Word Power® quiz book : over 1,000 word challenges
    from America's most popular magazine.
        p.   cm.
    ISBN 0-89577-822-X
    1. Vocabulary—Problems, exercises, etc.   I.Reader's digest.
    PE1449.R438   1995
    428.1—dc20   95-21922

Reader's Digest, Word Power® and the Pegasus logo are registered trademarks of The Reader's Digest Association, Inc.

Printed in the United States of America

Words sing. They hurt. They teach. They sanctify.

They were man's first, immeasurable feat of magic.

They liberated us from ignorance and our barbarous past.

—LEO ROSTEN

R*eader's Digest* has always been a magazine for people who seek to expand their horizons, to improve their abilities, to achieve their goals. No other feature exemplifies this better than "It Pays to Enrich Your Word Power." Over the years, it has come to be known as the department people turn to first, to diversify and enrich the words they use at home, in the classroom and in the workplace. Lee A. Iacocca, former chairman of the Chrysler Corporation, remembers that as a ninth-grader he was given vocabulary tests based on words from *Reader's Digest*. "Today, more than fifty years later, I always check out 'It Pays to Enrich Your Word Power' first when The Digest comes each month," Iacocca says. "I have learned that a word can work a small miracle—if it's the right word, in the right place, at the right time."

"The editors of 'Word Power' don't specify that the payment of a resourceful vocabulary is only in commercial mint," wrote William F. Buckley, Jr., on the fiftieth anniversary of the department's appearance in *Reader's Digest*. "The unusual word—if it fits exactly the meaning you want, if it is comfortably in rhythm with what comes before and after—repays the thought you gave to learning it by giving you pleasure, and by pleasing the person who hears it."

Fran Healy learned this lesson well. Some people were surprised in the late 1970s when this hardworking catcher for the New York Yankees made the smooth transition from ballplayer to professional sportscaster. They didn't know that for years, Healy's father had drilled his young son in vocabulary—using "Word Power" as a fun-filled teaching tool. Healy credits these challenges, in part, for his success as a broadcaster for the New York Mets.

Today, everyone is looking for the secret to achieving successful language skills. New audiotapes, videos and computer programs come and go, promising quick fixes and shortcuts to a better vocabulary.

But for more than fifty years, *Reader's Digest* has had the secret. There have been no gimmicks, no clever packaging, no shortcuts, no boring lectures: just "Word Power." One page of twenty words and eighty possible choices and another page of twenty answers. Seemingly so simple, yet so challenging.

If there is a key to "Word Power"'s success, that's it: the challenge. Everyone strives for the department's "Exceptional" ranking. Some achieve it, others do not. But each month, everyone returns, ready to try again. Readers of The Digest know that with "Word Power" a mistake is never a setback, it is simply another opportunity to learn.

Kenneth Y. Tomlinson
Editor-in-Chief
Reader's Digest

CONTENTS

M y friend Harry told me about a joke he'd played on his wife that demonstrates the power of a word.

"As company amanuensis, my wife, Mary, keeps the books at our company and answers most of the mail. During a recent vacation to Puerto Rico, my sense of humor soon led me into some word play. Anticipating that few in our group would know the definition of the word, I confided to some of the fellows in a low voice that I was vacationing with my amanuensis."

Harry laughed. "By the time the plane landed, Mary noticed, to her distress, that the women were avoiding her and the men looking at her with increased interest. I think they envied me and wished they dared to go off with an amanuensis. I was enjoying the joke so much, the ramifications didn't occur to me. Later Mary chatted with one of the wives about our eight grandchildren and our joy in them. The joke was over.

"When Mary realized what I'd done she was furious. 'And you didn't explain that an amanuensis is simply someone who writes letters and takes dictation?'

"I mollified her by saying that as a grandmother she should be proud to be taken for my amanuensis —whatever that word might have meant to those good people."

MY AFFLICTIVE SATURDAY MORNINGS:
The Origins of "Word Power"

My father, Wilfred Funk, would have relished this
story, for he knew well the power of words. Son of Dr.
I. K. Funk, a lexicographer who created Funk &
Wagnalls and the dictionary, he was a poet as well as
a lexicographer.

My father's initial inspiration for his books on
vocabulary building and the *Reader's Digest* feature
"It Pays to Enrich Your Word Power" came from his
fuming about the way schools taught vocabulary.
When I brought home a list of words to memorize
with their definitions, he'd shake his head in disgust.
"What an asinine way to treat words. How could anyone learn to love words without knowing something
about them, how they're used or where they've come
from? It's a crime against our exquisite language."

Words held a magical wonder for him. They
represented the culmination of civilization, each in
some way a repository of the past. He'd marvel at the
appearance of every new scientific term that might
quickly spawn a dozen other words. He described
words until they shimmered with the excitement
of life.

Even so, I dreaded Saturday mornings. My
brother, sisters, and I became my father's vocabulary-
building guinea pigs, and every Saturday morning
after breakfast he would try out various vocabulary

tests on us. But this was Saturday! I had other things on my mind than taking tests. His enthusiasm, however, eventually ensnared me. I began to see words through my father's eyes and to become fascinated by what he called these Alice in Wonderland creatures.

Later he wrote the pioneering vocabulary builder *30 Days to a More Powerful Vocabulary*. It became a bestseller and the prototype of the flood of vocabulary builders that followed.

In 1944 he worked up a word quiz with an inspiring introduction and took it to DeWitt Wallace, founder and editor-in-chief of *Reader's Digest*. With keen editorial insight Mr. Wallace foresaw the phenomenal popularity it would have among *Reader's Digest* readers, not only in the U.S. but around the world. The feature appeared in the January 1945 issue. I've written it since 1965.

David Crystal, an English lecturer, writer, and broadcaster on linguistics, said of "Word Power" that "the world-famous page from *Reader's Digest* has persuaded several generations of readers to take an interest in their vocabulary."

INCREASING WORD POWER
DEVELOPS BRAIN POWER

My many years as a lexical semanticist (a scholar who studies the meaning of words) have led me to adapt Wittgenstein's observation to my own experience: The limits of the size and quality of our vocabulary form the limits of our minds. And I especially stress quality over sheer size.

For example, concept words are quality words having to do with ideas. They stimulate us to think in new ways. *Integrity* is a concept word, as are *heuristic*, *reify*, *entropy*, *revelation*, *coalesce*, *dissident* and *compassion*. All of these words are found in the various tests in this book.

Whenever we learn a new word, it is not just dumped into our "mental dictionary." Our brain creates neuron connections between the new word and others relevant to our interests. It develops new perceptions and concepts.

HOW LARGE IS LARGE?

What is the size of your vocabulary? It has been estimated that a high school graduate may know up to 25,000 words, a college graduate up to 50,000. Yet our actual vocabularies are difficult to assess. Take the words *run, running,* and *ran*. Are *running* and *ran* simply different forms of *run*? Or do they constitute a vocabulary of three words? Today most lexical semanticists choose to count only the basic form of the word.

According to David Crystal in *The Cambridge Encyclopedia of the English Language* "[the size of one's vocabulary] depends on a person's hobbies and educational background. Someone who reads several novels a week is obviously going to pick up a larger vocabulary than someone whose daily reading is restricted to the telephone directory. And a degree in chemistry or botany will result in an enormous increase in (a specialized) vocabulary." Such a scientific vocabulary, however, is not of much use in ordinary communication.

From my work on "It Pays to Enrich Your Word Power," I estimate that, eliminating highly technical words employed by relatively few people, the essential English language we use to communicate with each other consists of about 15,000 words.

GETTING TO KNOW YOU

I find it frustrating to learn a new word and then, when it's just the one I need, to be unable to recall it. Here are a few helpful tips.

Make flash cards on which to write new words, with illustrations of their usage. Include origins, for they can be an aid to remembering a word. Add one or two of the closest synonyms from the thesaurus to gain a sense of the word's range.

For the first week or so, use these words as often as possible in your speaking and writing.

Get the best dictionary. If you can afford it, buy two: a desk edition and an unabridged both in the most recent versions available. You need the latest guide to our ever-changing language.

Another volume to have is a thesaurus. English, more than any other language, has vast numbers of synonyms. A synonym gives a slightly different slant to the meaning of a word, adding precision to your thinking and communicating. A synonym is to a writer or speaker what a shade of color is to a painter.

WHAT "WORD POWER" WILL DO FOR YOU

Brain experts claim that your ability to learn can remain steady throughout your life. And what do they point to as one of the surest and most enjoyable ways to expand your brain power? Enriching your word power. These quizzes will be a powerful aid in this endeavor.

• You will learn a myriad of new words. You will also refresh your memory of those words that you know but haven't used for a while.

• You will discover how certain words relate to the lives and thoughts of famous personalities.

• You will read about the fascinating etymologies that add so much to word lore.

• You will find a host of words that are relative newcomers to the English language. The English language has never been on a leash. It has roamed freely, returning home with "friends" from all over the world, from science, technology, various ethnic groups and other nations and cultures.

Most of all, our hope is that you will find a new enthusiasm for adding to your "word power" and that this book will bring greater richness and pleasure to your life.

—Peter Funk

"In the beginning was the word." Logos, *the Greek term originally used for "word" in this Bible verse from the New Testament, and its Latin counter-*part loqui, *have given birth to numerous words. Each word in this quiz derives from one or the other. Select the answer you think is correct. Turn the page for your score.*

ventriloquism *n.* — A: repetition of words. B: method of recording. C: "throwing" one's voice. D: speech impairment.

loquacious *adj.* — A: evasive. B: multilingual. C: unctuous. D: talkative.

monologue *n.* — A: long speech. B: scholarly work. C: editorial. D: hum.

terminology *n.* — A: nomenclature. B: extremity. C: mannerism. D: grammar.

elocution *n.* — A: deprecation. B: oratory. C: appeal. D: legalese.

interlocutor *n.* — A: go-between. B: researcher. C: dialogist. D: translator.

tautology (taw TAHL uh jee) *n.* — A: consistency in reasoning. B: careful instruction. C: nervousness. D: unnecessary repetition.

eulogy (YOO luh jee) *n.* — A: formal praise. B: commencement address. C: promise. D: sorrowful poem.

apologist *n.* — someone who A: broods on the past. B: makes no excuses. C: is fearful. D: defends an idea.

prologue *n.* — A: introduction. B: explication. C: game plan. D: précis.

"Speak the truth, but leave immediately after. **"**

—SLOVENIAN PROVERB

> **"** Talking is like playing the harp; there is as much in laying the hands on the strings to stop their vibrations as in twanging them to bring out their music. **"**
>
> —OLIVER WENDELL HOLMES, SR.

---

philology (fuh LOL uh jee) *n.* — study of A: basic truths. B: races and cultures. C: nonverbal language. D: literary texts.

Decalogue *n.* — A: famous series of plays. B: Ten Commandments. C: type of exile. D: permanent record.

lexicologist *n.* — one who A: announces sports. B: trains birds to speak. C: writes letters.
D: studies word meanings and origins.

analogy *n.* — A: detailed examination. B: partial similarity.
C: newly coined word. D: figure of speech.

logophile *n.* — lover of A: words. B: books. C: trademarks.
D: sermons.

dialogue *n.* — A: argument. B: instruction. C: conversation.
D: lecture.

circumlocution *n.* — A: faux pas. B: search. C: innuendo.
D: verbosity.

sinologist *n.* — expert in A: origins of evil. B: Chinese civilization.
C: sign language. D: head colds.

cosmology *n.* — study of A: the universe. B: plastic surgery.
C: city life. D: earth's surface.

epilogue *n.* — A: comedy. B: plot line. C: concluding statement.
D: beginning of a story.

 *ANSWERS*

ventriloquism — C: "Throwing" one's voice; Latin *ventriloquus* (one who speaks from the belly).

loquacious — D: A mildly disparaging term for being talkative or wordy; as, a *loquacious* salesman. Latin *loqui* (to speak).

monologue — A: Long speech by a single speaker, monopolizing a conversation; dramatic speech by one actor. Greek *monologos* (speaking alone).

terminology — A: Nomenclature; technical terms relating to a specific subject. Latin *terminus* (limit) and Greek *logos* (word, speech).

elocution — B: Oratory; style or manner of speaking or reading in public. Latin *eloqui* (to speak out).

interlocutor — C: Dialogist; person who takes part in a conversation or discussion and who may ask questions; as, The journalist was a skilled *interlocutor*. Latin *interloqui* (to speak between).

tautology — D: Unnecessary repetition of an idea in different words. Greek *tauto* (the same) and *logos*.

eulogy — A: Formal praise of a person, especially one who has died recently. Greek *eulogia* (praise).

apologist — D: One who explains or defends an idea, cause or person; as, an *apologist* for tough laws against drug dealers. Greek *apologia* (speech in defense).

prologue — A: Introduction to a poem, play, book, etc.; preliminary event; as, The conference of American and Russian negotiators was a *prologue* to a summit meeting. Greek *pro-* (for) and *logos*.

philology — D: Study of literary texts and written records to determine their authenticity and meaning. Greek *philein* (to love) and *logos*.

Decalogue — B: The Ten Commandments. Greek *deka* (ten) and *logos*.

lexicologist — D: One who studies the formation of words and their derivations, meanings and uses. Greek *lexikos* (of words) and *logos*.

analogy — B: Partial similarity of things unlike in various aspects but forming a basis for comparison; as, the *analogy* of a human lung to a balloon. Greek *ana* (similar to) and *logos*.

logophile — A: Lover of words; as, Many of you who read this feature are *logophiles*. Greek *logos* and *philos* (loving).

dialogue — C: Conversation; especially a frank exchange of different points of view. Greek *dialogos*.

circumlocution — D: Verbosity; roundabout way of speaking or writing; as, Come to the point. Don't use *circumlocutions*. Latin *circum-* (around) and *loqui*.

sinologist — B: An expert in Chinese language, literature, history, art and customs. Greek *Sinai* (the Chinese people) and *logos*.

cosmology — A: The study of the nature, origin, structure and evolution of the universe. Greek *kosmos* (universe) and *logos*.

epilogue — C: Concluding statement of a novel or play, giving further insight; as, the *epilogue* spoken by Prospero in Shakespeare's *The Tempest*. Greek *epilogos*.

Vocabulary Ratings
  9 — 11 correct . . . Good
  12 — 17 correct . . . Excellent
  18 — 20 correct . . . Exceptional

EUPHUNISMS
Cheap: fiscally retentive

Crooked: ethically challenged —Constance Brancato

Old: chronologically gifted
—George O. Ludcke in *The Wall Street Journal*

LATIN LIVES ON

Latin is enjoying a revival in many schools today. Since more than half of our English words derive from Latin, in a sense we speak it every day. Bring the following words and phrases to life. Turn the page to find your score.

nonplussed — A: displeased. B: diminished. C: dumbfounded. D: blocked.

terra firma — A: fright. B: determination. C: solid ground. D: indecision.

bona fide — A: with optimism. B: free. C: costly. D: in good faith.

nota bene (NO tuh BAY nay) — A: to act generously. B: note well. C: ignore. D: bless.

alter ego — A: foe. B: other self. C: honored mentor. D: uncertainty.

in loco parentis (in LO ko puh REN tis) — A: eccentric parents. B: in place of a parent. C: in a safe place. D: in quest of a place.

persona non grata — a person who is A: lacking in manners. B: unacceptable. C: not responsible. D: ungrateful.

caveat emptor (KAH vee at EMP tor) — A: ignore hunger. B: let the buyer beware. C: first come, first served. D: never give up.

sub rosa — A: beautifully. B: carefully. C: secretly. D: colorfully.

per diem (per DEE um) — A: over and over again. B: for the moment. C: gradually. D: by the day.

per se (per SAY) — A: as if. B: just the way it is. C: because. D: by or in itself.

❝If you have a garden and a library, you have everything you need.**❞**

—*Cicero*

> **"**Fable is more historical than fact, because fact tells us about one man and fable tells us about a million men.**"**
>
> *—G. K. Chesterton*

---

sine qua non (SIH neh kwah NOHN) — A: everything is gone. B: out of sight, out of mind. C: without which there is nothing. D: mentally unsound.

et al. — A: altogether. B: the end. C: and others. D: there are no leftovers.

ad nauseam — A: to a sickening degree. B: uncouth. C: evil. D: foul-smelling.

in extremis (in ek STREE miss) — A: the nearest site. B: stretched to the limit. C: at the point of death. D: disgraced.

in vitro (in VEE tro) — A: dipped in wine. B: fully alive. C: according to law. D: artificially maintained.

modus operandi (MOH dus op uh RAN dee) — A: way of working. B: big-time operator. C: sense of the future. D: international agreement.

ex officio (eks uh FISH ee oh) — A: formerly. B: out of office. C: unofficially. D: by virtue of office.

quid pro quo — A: something for nothing. B: easy come, easy go. C: in payment of. D: something for something.

status quo — A: existing condition. B: precedent. C: sum total. D: decree.

> **"**A different language is a different vision of life.**"**
>
> *—Federico Fellini, quoted by Mary Cantwell in New York Times*

 *ANSWERS*

nonplussed — C: Dumbfounded. When *nonplussed*, we are so stunned that we temporarily can't act or think. *Non-* (not) and *plus* (more).

terra firma — C: Solid ground; as, Back on the dock, the seasick passenger said, "Am I glad to be on *terra firma!*"

bona fide — D: In good faith; sincere; genuine; as, He made a *bona fide* offer for the beach cottage.

nota bene — B: Note well or observe. Usually abbreviated as *N.B.* and used to call attention to something; as, *N.B.* Appointment of this judge will have a lasting effect.

alter ego — B: Other self; perfect substitute; intimate friend; as, Her husband became her *alter ego*.

in loco parentis — B: In the place or role of a parent; as, The university stated it would not act *in loco parentis* for freshmen.

persona non grata — B: A person unacceptable or not welcome; as, The attaché's deception made him *persona non grata* (especially said of a foreign diplomat not acceptable to the host government).

caveat emptor — B: Let the buyer beware; as, When purchasing a used car, remember: *caveat emptor*.

sub rosa — C: Secretly; confidentially; as, to pass on information *sub rosa*.

per diem — D: By the day; daily allowance for expenses; as, The traveling salesman was given a fixed *per diem*.

per se — D: By or in itself; intrinsically; belonging to the basic nature of a person or thing; as, The writer was not a scholar *per se* and made many loose generalizations.

sine qua non — C: Without which there is nothing; indispensable requirement; something essential; as, Love is the *sine qua non* of human existence.

et al. — C: And others; abbreviation of Latin *et alii*; as, my law firm of Harris, Dickson *et al*.

ad nauseam — A: To a sickening or disgusting degree; as, They complained about anything and everything *ad nauseam*.

in extremis — C: At the point of death; in extremity; as, The searchers found the fallen rock climber *in extremis*.

in vitro — D: Artificially maintained in a controlled environment; as, a test-tube baby conceived when an ovum is fertilized *in vitro*. Literally "in glass."

modus operandi — A: Way of working; procedure; as, to discuss a *modus operandi* for future space shots.

ex officio — D: By virtue of office or because of one's position; as, Having expertise in finance, she served *ex officio* on the committee.

quid pro quo — D: Something for something; one thing given in return for another of similar value; as, The negotiator demanded a *quid pro quo*.

status quo — A: Existing condition or situation; as, He was reluctant to disturb the *status quo*.

Vocabulary Ratings
     9 — 11 correct . . . Good
     12 — 17 correct . . . Excellent
     18 — 20 correct . . . Exceptional

❝He who does not prevent a crime when he can, encourages it.**❞**

—*SENECA*

STRAIGHT TALK

Businessman and author Lee Iacocca is a straight talker who knows how to pack a wallop with his words. He began building his vocabulary early by reading "Word Power" and exchanging verbal spars with his classmates. Here are some of Iacocca's choice words. How much mileage can you get out of them? Turn the page to find out.

aspire v. — A: to animate. B: aim for. C: end. D: pretend.

meddlesome adj. — A: spirited. B: fretful. C: interfering. D: fainthearted.

albatross n. — sea bird symbolizing A: persistent difficulty. B: ecstasy. C: effortless achievement. D: lost treasure.

permeate v. — A: to firm up. B: rearrange. C: force an opening into. D: spread through.

consortium (kun SOR she um) n. — A: monopoly. B: partnership. C: illegal transaction. D: rental unit.

laissez-faire (LEH say fair) adj. — A: easy come, easy go. B: at rest. C: unregulated. D: harmonious.

divisive adj. — A: dishonest. B: roundabout. C: candid. D: disruptive.

ad hoc adj. — A: for this purpose. B: unreal. C: possible. D: confidential.

harbor v. — A: to encourage. B: keep in one's mind. C: reinforce. D: lose sight of.

❝ Not the fastest horse can catch a word spoken in anger. **❞**

—CHINESE PROVERB

66 The real art of conversation is not only to say the right thing in the right place, but to leave unsaid the wrong thing at the tempting moment. **99**

---

tout (TOWT) *v.* — A: to oppose. B: suppress. C: deceive. D: praise.
catharsis *n.* — A: result. B: intensity. C: weakness. D: purification.
envisage (en VIZ ij) *v.* — A: to visualize. B: plan for. C: idealize.
D: surround.
contentious *adj.* — A: relevant or pertinent. B: controversial. C: full. D: quiet.
exacerbate (eg ZAS uhr bate) *v.* — A: to analyze carefully. B: make worse. C: uncover. D: argue.
rag *v.* — A: to humiliate. B: challenge. C: tease. D: clean up.
watershed *n.* — A: fluid situation. B: protective arrangement. C: small waterfall. D: decisive turning point.
reparation *n.* — A: making up for a wrongdoing.
B: severe punishment. C: a pulling apart. D: redistribution.
homogenize *v.* — A: to weaken. B: blend. C: adapt. D: separate.
faze *v.* — A: to fluster. B: fade away. C: dominate. D: gloss over.
temper *v.* — A: to drive to distraction. B: synchronize. C: mold.
D: moderate.

---

66 Many people who have the gift of gab don't know how to wrap it up. **99**

—ARNOLD H. GLASOW

Straight Talk • 25

aspire — B: To aim for something important; be ambitious; yearn for. Latin *aspirare* (to breathe upon).

meddlesome — C: Interfering; inclined to pry intrusively into the lives of others; as, a *meddlesome* reporter. Old French *medler* (to mix).

albatross — A: Persistent difficulty or burden. From Coleridge's poem in which a ship's crew hung a dead *albatross* around the Ancient Mariner's neck. Sailors believed that killing this bird brought bad luck.

permeate — D: To spread through every part of; as, A feeling of relief *permeated* the company. Latin *permeare* (to pass through).

consortium — B: Partnership of financial groups for carrying out a large project; as, an international *consortium* of car companies. Latin (fellowship).

laissez-faire — C: Unregulated; often used to describe an economic system free of government control. French (let do).

divisive — D: Disruptive; causing disagreement among people; as, their *divisive* statements. Latin *dividere* (to divide).

ad hoc — A: For a specific purpose only; as, an *ad hoc* investigative committee. Latin (for this).

harbor — B: To keep or hold in one's mind; as, to *harbor* resentments. Old English *herebeorg* (army shelter).

tout — D: To praise or recommend highly; as, He believed in the cars he *touted*. Old English *totian* (to look out for).

catharsis — D: Purification; a cleansing; as, Some contend that business recessions are a necessary *catharsis* for an economic system. Greek *katharsis*.

envisage — A: To visualize; imagine; as, to *envisage* a new organization. French *envisager* (to face in).

contentious — B: Controversial; causing argument; as, quarrelsome; the most *contentious* person imaginable. Latin *com-* (with) and *tendere* (to strive).

exacerbate — B: To make worse; aggravate; as, to *exacerbate* a weak financial situation. Latin *ex-* (thoroughly) and *acerbare* (to make harsh).

rag — C: To tease, banter or joke in an annoyingly persistent way; as, Our competitor *ragged* us. British 19th-century university slang.

watershed — D: Decisive turning point affecting outlook, actions; as, The merger was a *watershed* in the firm's history. Also, area from which a river receives its water supply.

reparation — A: Making up for a wrongdoing; amends; as, to make *reparations* by a public apology. Also, compensation. Latin *re-* (again) and *parare* (to get ready).

homogenize — B: To blend diverse elements into a smooth, uniform mixture; as, It can be dangerous to *homogenize* one's thinking. Greek *homogenes* (of the same kind).

faze — A: To fluster; disturb or intimidate; as, Nothing *fazed* him. Middle English *fesen*.

temper — D: To moderate; soften effects of; as, to *temper* a government regulation. Latin *temperare* (to keep within limits).

Vocabulary Ratings
> 9 — 11 correct . . . Good
> 12 — 17 correct . . . Excellent
> 18 — 20 correct . . . Exceptional

❝One of the most dangerous forms of human error is forgetting what one is trying to achieve.**❞**

—PAUL NITZE

WORDS TO BANK ON

The following words come from various press commentaries on the banking industry's difficulties. How many of these words can you "bank" on? Mark the answer you think is correct. Turn the page to find your score.

consolidate *v.* — A: to complete. B: distribute. C: combine. D: offer.

legal tender *n.* — A: laundered money. B: intrabank transaction. C: legitimate currency. D: credit.

arrears (ah REARZ) *n.* — A: privileged knowledge. B: missing inventory. C: extended loan. D: unpaid, overdue debt.

mature *adj.* — A: past due. B: excessive. C: inactive. D: payable.

promissory note *n.* — A: written promise. B: mortgage. C: stock certificate. D: favorable loan.

roll over *v.* — A: to refinance. B: relax laws. C: negotiate favorably. D: be passive.

point *n.* — A: lease. B: bonus to borrower. C: late-payment penalty. D: prepaid interest.

redundant *adj.* — A: scarce. B: overabundant. C: increasing. D: stagnant.

demand deposit *n.* — A: short-term loan. B: mortgage payment. C: checking account. D: reinvestment of interest.

voucher *n.* — A: document proving payment. B: statement of financial condition. C: account book. D: withdrawal of money.

❝Never marry for money. Ye'll borrow it cheaper. **❞**

—Scottish proverb

> **"**Finance is the art of passing currency from hand to hand until it finally disappears.**"**
>
> —ROBERT W. SARNOFF, QUOTED BY MALCOLM S. FORBES, SR., IN FORBES

---

convertible *adj.* — A: inconsistent. B: exchangeable. C: shoddy. D: collectible.

liquid assets *n.* — valuables that are A: of a floating value. B: volatile. C: suddenly worthless. D: in cash.

debacle *n.* — A: complication. B: trickery. C: evil. D: collapse.

par value *n.* — A: face amount. B: average cost. C: market equivalent. D: worth at sale.

conveyance *n.* — A: compromise. B: legal brief. C: property survey. D: deed.

ire (EYE 'r) *n.* — A: pride. B: pity. C: determination. D: anger.

lien (LEAN) *n.* — A: legal claim. B: false statement. C: stock offering. D: sales invoice.

compound interest *n.* — interest paid on A: principal. B: bonds. C: principal and unpaid interest. D: stocks.

fungible (FUN juh b'l) *adj.* — A: expendable. B: interchangeable. C: dated. D: mildewed.

sacred cow *n.* — anything thought of as A: above criticism. B: unusual. C: well-heeled. D: showy or pompous.

FROM BAD TO VERSE

A bookkeeper, asked to explain
How his fortunes made gain after gain
Said he'd rather not tell
But now he's in a cell—
It was bookkeeping ledger-de-main

—LOUIS HASLEY

 *ANSWERS*

consolidate — C: To combine separate units into a whole. Latin *consolidare* (to make firm).

legal tender — C: Currency that cannot lawfully be refused in payment of an obligation. Latin *legis* (law) and *tendere* (to extend, offer).

arrears — D: Unpaid, overdue debt or obligation; as, Her mortgage payment was two months in *arrears*. Middle English *arrere* (behind).

mature — D: Payable or due; as, a note, loan or bond that becomes *mature*. Latin *maturus* (at full age).

promissory note — A: Written promise to pay a debt at a designated date or on demand. Latin *promissor* (one who promises) and *nota* (mark or sign).

roll over — A: To refinance a maturing obligation by offering a new one of the same type in exchange. Also, to reinvest funds as IRAs or CDs.

point — D: Interest fee, equal to one percent of the loan amount, that is deducted in advance by the lender. As, Many banks no longer charge *points* in granting a mortgage. Latin *punctum* (dot).

redundant — B: Overabundant; more than is needed; as, weeding out *redundant* banks. Latin *redundare* (to overflow).

demand deposit — C: Checking account or similar deposit that may be withdrawn without notice. Latin *demandare* (to entrust) and *deponere* (to put down).

voucher — A: Document proving payment; as, The salesman handed the hotel clerk his room *voucher*. Latin *vocare* (to call).

convertible — B: Exchangeable for something of equal value; as, a *convertible* bond, which on maturity becomes exchangeable for the equivalent in shares of common stock. Latin *convertere* (to turn around).

liquid assets — D: Valuables that are in cash or otherwise quickly convertible into cash. Latin *liquere* (to be fluid) and French *assez* (enough).

debacle — D: Disastrous collapse; humiliating failure; as, The savings-and-loan crisis was a national *debacle*. French *debacler* (to break up).

par value — A: Face amount of a security at the time of issue; as, The bank's holdings were under *par value*. Latin *par* (equal) and *valere* (to be worth).

conveyance — D: Deed; transference of property ownership, especially as real estate. Latin *conviare*.

ire — D: Anger; as, Unscrupulous savings-and-loan operators raised his *ire*. Latin *ira*.

lien — A: Legal claim to take, hold or sell property of a person who owes money; as, a *lien* on a builder's assets. Latin *ligare* (to bind).

compound interest — C: Interest paid on both principal and the accumulated unpaid interest. Latin *componere* (to put together) and *interesse*.

fungible — B: Interchangeable and equivalent in value to satisfy an obligation; as, Gold bullion and the equivalent dollars are *fungible*. Latin *fungi* (to perform).

sacred cow — A: Anything thought of as above, or immune to, criticism; as, Many people thought of banks as *sacred cows*. From the Hindu practice of venerating cows.

Vocabulary Ratings
- 9 — 11 correct . . . Good
- 12 — 17 correct . . . Excellent
- 18 — 20 correct . . . Exceptional

66Money is flat and meant to be piled up.**99**

—*SCOTTISH PROVERB*

EN ROUTE

Just as a propeller drives a ship ahead, the "fy" ending on a word impels it forward. "Fy" comes from the Latin facere *(to make). Turn the page to find out if these twenty verbs have helped you move forward on your route to a larger, more effective vocabulary.*

certify — A: to verify. B: claim. C: issue a license. D: list.

vilify — A: to shame. B: slander. C: confront. D: lie.

personify — A: to popularize. B: be friendly. C: state boldly.
D: typify.

amplify — A: to satisfy. B: round off. C: increase. D: prolong.

indemnify (in DEM nih fy) — A: to accuse. B: bring to trial.
C: protect. D: challenge or oppose.

stultify — A: to be stubborn. B: make ineffective. C: harden.
D: shrink to unusable size.

quantify — A: to measure. B: empower. C: excuse oneself.
D: add to.

stupefy — A: to strengthen. B: frustrate. C: cripple. D: dull.

codify — A: to translate. B: make firm. C: systematize. D: explain.

deify — A: to commemorate. B: idealize. C: preserve.
D: exaggerate.

exemplify (egg ZEM plih fy) — A: to discuss. B: imitate.
C: illustrate. D: punish.

66Determine that the thing can and shall be done, and
then we shall find the way.**99**

—ABRAHAM LINCOLN

66He that would be a leader must be a bridge.**99**

—WELSH PROVERB

---

sanctify — A: to consecrate. B: become quiet. C: be in seclusion.
    D: grow in religious fervor.
transmogrify (trans MOG rih fy) — A: to transform. B: be in a hypnotic sleep. C: disintegrate. D: be in distress.
nullify — A: to retreat. B: even out. C: question. D: cancel.
reify (REE ih fy) — A: to make louder. B: reinforce continually.
    C: treat an abstract as a tangible. D: become more elegant.
justify — A: to put into law. B: substantiate. C: quibble about.
    D: gloss over.
mortify — A: to humiliate. B: exasperate. C: exterminate.
    D: give in to.
minify — A: to lessen. B: extend. C: calm. D: work carefully.
gentrify — A: to impoverish. B: farm as a hobby. C: upgrade.
    D: be excessively polite.
edify — A: to admire. B: uplift. C: enjoy. D: be diligent.

ROAD SHOWS

On outskirts of small town: "Welcome, speeders! We're policed
to meet you!"

—LEONARD BOSSARD

"Cross road ahead—better humor it."

—BENNETT CERF

On a marquee: "Don't learn traffic laws by accident."

—HILDEGARDE REVAK

certify — A: To verify; confirm as true and accurate; guarantee; as, to have a bank teller *certify* that the signature is yours. Latin *certus* (certain).

vilify — B: To slander; make vicious statements about; blacken a good name; as, The surprise witness lied and *vilified* the two defendants. Latin *vilis* (cheap, base).

personify — D: To typify; represent; embody; as, To her students, Miss Rodgers *personified* the ideal teacher. Old French *persone* (person).

amplify — C: To increase or make stronger; as, The floods *amplified* the earthquake's devastation. Also, to add details or illustrations for clarity. Latin *amplus* (large).

indemnify — C: To protect against future damage; insure; as, to *indemnify* oneself against a car accident. Also, to compensate for loss. Latin *indemnis* (uninjured).

stultify — B: To make ineffective; impair; reduce to futility; as, Over-reliance on rote drill can *stultify* a student's ability to learn. Latin *stultus* (foolish).

quantify — A: To measure; determine or indicate the extent of; as, to try to *quantify* the amount of pollution in the air. Latin *quantus* (how much).

stupefy — D: To dull, stun or daze from shock, fatigue or narcotics; as, News of the disaster *stupefied* the victims' relatives. Also, to amaze. Latin *stupere* (to be stunned).

codify — C: To systematize laws, rules or regulations into a collection or code; as, to *codify* a town's building regulations. Latin *codex* (tablet on which laws were written).

deify — B: To idealize; exalt; glorify; make a god of; as, rock stars *deified* by their fans. Latin *deus* (god).

exemplify — C: To illustrate; show or serve as an example; as, *Tom Sawyer* is a novel that *exemplifies* small-town 19th-century American life. Medieval Latin *exemplum* (example).

sanctify — A: To consecrate; set apart as holy; as, to *sanctify* a burial ground. Also, to give religious sanction to, as in marriage vows. Latin *sanctus* (holy).

transmogrify — A: To transform; change completely in a fantastic or grotesque way; as, Dr. Jekyll was *transmogrified* into the monstrous Mr. Hyde. Origin unknown.

nullify — D: To cancel; annul; make legally void; as, to *nullify* an agreement. Also, to make useless; as, New technologies often *nullify* older styles of management. Latin *nullus* (none).

reify — C: To treat an abstraction as if it had a concrete or tangible existence; as, Some physicists *reify* the concept of spacetime. Latin *res* (thing).

justify — B: To substantiate; vindicate; as, to *justify* a budget. Also, to defend or absolve; as, Don't *justify* her rudeness. Latin *justus* (just, fair).

mortify — A: To humiliate greatly; cause shame or wounded pride; as, The spelling-bee winner was *mortified* by confusing "principle" with "principal." Latin *mors* (death).

minify — A: To lessen; reduce in size or importance; as, Never *minify* their contribution. Latin *min* (less).

gentrify — C: To upgrade a neighborhood by renovating homes; as, to *gentrify* the Independence Hall area of Philadelphia. English *gentry*.

edify — B: To uplift; encourage intellectual, moral and spiritual growth; as, Good books can *edify* the mind. Latin *aedes* (dwelling).

Vocabulary Ratings
        9 — 11 correct . . . Good
        12 — 17 correct . . . Excellent
        18 — 20 correct . . . Exceptional

EUREKA!

Bright ideas depend above all on a strong vocabulary to give them lasting brilliance. How many of the following words light up your face with understanding? Turn the page for your results.

resolve *n.* — A: self-reliance. B: willfulness. C: determination. D: protest.

comprehend *v.* — A: to examine. B: puzzle over. C: grasp mentally. D: consider.

premise *n.* — A: summary. B: pledge. C: proven fact. D: assumption.

demonstrable *adj.* — A: overwhelming. B: emotional. C: showy. D: evident.

reflective *adj.* — A: thoughtful. B: slow. C: responsive. D: watchful.

plausible (PLAW zih b'l) *adj.* — A: easily changed. B: seemingly true. C: authoritative. D: effective.

scrutiny *n.* — A: angry glance. B: cleanliness. C: caution. D: close examination.

envision *v.* — A: to explain. B: remember. C: imagine. D: encompass.

affirmation *n.* — A: firmness. B: dissension. C: approbation. D: confirmation.

practicable *adj.* — A: feasible. B: businesslike. C: experimental. D: influential.

curriculum *n.* — A: scheme or method. B: courses of study. C: end point. D: resource.

❝Education is not the filling of a pail, but the lighting of a fire.**❞**

—WILLIAM BUTLER YEATS

infrastructure (IN fruh struk chur) *n.* — A: foundation. B: political action committee. C: separation of powers. D: insiders' group.

initiate *v.* — A: to check off. B: review. C: begin. D: be enthusiastic.

inference *n.* — A: concept. B: accusation. C: representation. D: reasoned conclusion.

optimal *adj.* — A: promising. B: best. C: not compulsory. D: harmless.

sagacious (suh GAY shus) *adj.* — A: wise. B: heroic. C: fair-minded. D: elderly.

compensatory *adj.* — A: counterbalancing. B: regulated. C: punishing. D: unjust.

impasse *n.* — A: impractical condition. B: confrontation. C: bewilderment. D: stalemate.

probity (PRO buh tee) *n.* — A: procedure. B: honesty. C: legislative inquiry. D: self-righteousness.

lucid *adj.* — A: easily understood. B: colorful. C: without sense. D: highly intelligent.

 *ANSWERS*

resolve — C: Determination; firmness of purpose; as, She kept to her *resolve*. Latin *resolvere* (to unfasten, loosen).

comprehend — C: To grasp mentally; understand; as, He failed to *comprehend* the importance of the concept. Latin *comprehendere* (to grasp).

premise — D: Assumption; proposition or belief taken for granted but not proved; as, a strategy based on a faulty *premise*. Latin *praemittere* (to send before).

demonstrable — D: Clearly evident; able to be shown or authenticated; as, a *demonstrable* need to improve the quality of education. Latin *demonstrare* (to indicate).

reflective — A: Thoughtful; analytical; pensive; as, *Reflective* parents often avoid hasty reactions to their unruly children. Latin *reflectere* (to bend back).

plausible — B: Seemingly true or reasonable, though more proof is desirable; as, He gave *plausible* reasons for the change in plans. Latin *plaudere* (to applaud).

scrutiny — D: Close examination or searching study; as, The proposal is under the committee's *scrutiny*. Latin *scrutari* (to search).

envision — C: To imagine or picture in the mind, especially a future event; as, to *envision* a world at peace. English *en-* (cause) and *vision*.

affirmation — D: Confirmation or assertion that something is true; as, an *affirmation* of serious plans to reduce the deficit. Latin *affirmare* (to present as firm).

practicable — A: Feasible; capable of being done or put into practice; as, a *practicable* economic policy. Greek *praktikos* (practical).

curriculum — B: Courses of study offered in schools; as, to change a school's *curriculum*. Latin (a running contest).

infrastructure — A: Foundation; basic facilities needed for the functioning of a system, as a community's roads, schools or transportation system. Latin *infra* (below) and *structure*.

initiate — C: To begin; originate; as, to *initiate* reforms in Congress. Also, to teach the fundamentals of a subject. Latin *initiare*.

inference — D: Conclusion arrived at by reasoning based on known facts. Latin *inferre* (to bring in).

optimal — B: Best or most favorable; as, an *optimal* timing for the summit meeting. Latin *optimus*.

sagacious — A: Wise; having a keenly perceptive mind, good judgment and sound, practical sense; as, a *sagacious* judge. Latin *sagire* (to perceive quickly).

compensatory — A: Counterbalancing; making up for a loss; as, *compensatory* payment for damages. Latin *compensare*.

impasse — D: Stalemate; any deadlock; as, International trade negotiations failed to break the *impasse*. French.

probity — B: Uncompromising honesty; proven integrity; as, a beloved queen known for her *probity*. Latin *probus*.

lucid — A: Easily understood; clearly expressed; as, *lucid* instructions. Latin *lucere* (to shine, glitter).

Vocabulary Ratings
> 9 — 11 correct . . . Good
> 12 — 17 correct . . . Excellent
> 18 — 20 correct . . . Exceptional

❝The difference between the impossible and the possible lies in a person's determination.**❞**

—TOMMY LASORDA

NAMES THAT LAST

Want to make yourself immortal? Get your name published in the dictionary—as did Louis Braille and Captain Charles C. Boycott, among others. Their names have become eponyms—names synonymous with an invention, action or product. How many of these do you recognize? Turn the page for answers and your score.

dunce *n.* — person who is A: disobedient. B: spry. C: dull-witted. D: innocent.

ampere *n.* — unit for measuring A: electricity. B: water flow. C: light. D: heat.

leotard *n.* — A: headband. B: ballet slipper. C: close-fitting garment. D: long silk scarf.

mausoleum *n.* — A: Turkish rug. B: large urn. C: town square. D: tomb.

Annie Oakley *n.* — A: nonalcoholic drink. B: style of dress. C: free ticket. D: dilapidated auto.

maudlin (MAWD lin) *adj.* — A: forgetful. B: sensitive. C: gentle and kind. D: foolishly sentimental.

mesmerize *v.* — A: to polish. B: bewilder. C: daydream. D: hypnotize.

Lucullan (loo KUL UN) *adj.* — A: narrow-minded. B: widespread. C: light-filled. D: sumptuous.

chauvinistic (show vin IS tik) *adj.* — A: warm and friendly. B: manly. C: smug, superior in attitude. D: extremely stubborn.

shrapnel *n.* — A: perfume. B: shrub. C: scattered fragments. D: booster rocket.

❝The glory of great men should always be measured by the means they have used to acquire it.**❞**

—LA ROCHEFOUCAULD

CELEBRITY QUIZ

Will Donald Trump my ace? —Dorothy Damon

How many deals did Glenn Close? —Jean Wiggin

How did Tina Turner career around? —Chris Fisher and Ben MacKay

---

platonic *adj.* — A: ambitious. B: without envy. C: constant.
   D: spiritual or intellectual.

draconian *adj.* — A: horse-like. B: frightening. C: harsh. D: dreary.

Doppler effect *n.* — change in A: potency of a sedative.
   B: sound frequencies. C: tire traction. D: sleep patterns.

Caesarean *n.* — A: surgical procedure. B: political skill.
   C: leadership. D: winning attitude.

martinet *n.* — A: bird lover. B: hero. C: puppet.
   D: strict disciplinarian.

Pyrrhic (PEER ik) **victory** — one that is A: overwhelming.
   B: gained at great cost. C: quick. D: won by a few over many.

Machiavellian (mack ee ah VEL ee ahn) *adj.* — A: crafty. B: weird.
   C: straightforward. D: practical.

maverick *n.* — A: wanderer. B: sly cheat. C: nonconformist.
   D: loyal servant.

spoonerism *n.* — A: secret romance. B: slip of the tongue. C: hobby
   of collecting antiques. D: baby talk.

cardigan *n.* — A: emblem. B: open-front sweater. C: type of wool.
   D: skirt.

“No steam or gas drives anything until it is confined. No life
ever grows great until it is focused, dedicated, disciplined. **”**

—HARRY EMERSON FOSDICK, LIVING UNDER TENSION (HARPERCOLLINS)

ANSWERS

dunce — C: Dull-witted or ignorant person. Used by Renaissance humanists to ridicule followers of John *Duns* Scotus (1265?-1308), a Scottish theologian.

ampere — A: Standard unit for measuring the strength of electric current; as, a 15-*ampere* fuse. Named after French physicist André Marie *Ampère* (1775-1836).

leotard — C: Close-fitting, one-piece garment. After Jules *Léotard*, a 19th-century French aerialist.

mausoleum — D: Magnificent tomb; large, gloomy building. After the tomb for King *Mausolus*, fourth century B.C., one of the seven wonders of the ancient world.

Annie Oakley — C: Free ticket or pass. After *Annie Oakley* (1860-1926), an expert shot whose playing-card targets resembled punched tickets.

maudlin — D: Foolishly sentimental; emotional. Old French *Madeleine* for *Mary Magdalene*, a follower of Christ often portrayed as weeping.

mesmerize — D: To hypnotize, spellbind, enchant. After German physician Franz Anton *Mesmer* (1734-1815).

Lucullan — D: Sumptuous or lavish, usually pertaining to banquets; as, *Lucullan* meals on cruise ships. After Lucius Lucinius *Lucullus* (110?-57? B.C.), a Roman general famous for staging elaborate banquets.

chauvinistic — C: Smug, superior in attitude as to race, sex or nationality; as, *chauvinistic* women or men. Also, fanatically patriotic. From Nicolas *Chauvin*, a French soldier fiercely loyal to Napoleon.

shrapnel — C: Scattered fragments from an exploding shell or bomb. After Henry *Shrapnel* (1761-1842), a British artillery officer.

platonic — D: Spiritual or intellectual; nonsexual; especially as describes a close relationship between a man and a woman. After *Plato*, Greek philosopher (fourth century B.C.).

draconian — C: Very harsh; unusually severe or cruel; as, *draconian* punishment for dissenters. After *Draco*, Greek lawgiver (seventh century B.C.).

Doppler effect — B: Change in the pitch of sound, to higher frequencies when the source approaches and lower as it recedes, as with a train whistle. After Austrian physicist Christian *Doppler* (1803-53).

Caesarean — A: Surgical operation to deliver a baby — called a *Caesarean* section in medical terminology. From the folklore surrounding Julius *Caesar's* birth.

martinet — D: Strict disciplinarian; as, Our Marine Corps sergeant was a *martinet*. After the 17th-century French drillmaster Jean *Martinet*.

Pyrrhic victory — B: Victory achieved at such great cost that it is nearly a defeat. From the victory of *Pyrrhus*, king of Epirus, over the Romans (279 B.C.).

Machiavellian — A: Crafty, deceitful or amoral; as, *Machiavellian* political intrigue. After the Florentine writer Nicolò *Machiavelli* (1469-1527).

maverick — C: Nonconformist; person with unorthodox or independent views. After Samuel *Maverick* (1803-70), a Texas rancher who chose not to brand his cattle.

spoonerism — B: Slip of the tongue; as, calling a "well-oiled bicycle" a "well-boiled icicle." After the Rev. William A. *Spooner* (1844-1930), who was noted for such slips.

cardigan — B: Open-front sweater. After the seventh Earl of *Cardigan* (1797-1868), a British general.

Vocabulary Ratings

> 9 — 11 correct . . . Good
> 12 — 17 correct . . . Excellent
> 18 — 20 correct . . . Exceptional

WORLDS OF OPPORTUNITIES

Newly learned words can carry you, like a glider caught in an updraft, to greater heights of understanding. The following terms are drawn from news of economic opportunities opened up by recent world changes. Select the answers you think are correct, then turn the page for your score.

ethic *n.* — A: standard of behavior. B: racial group. C: precision. D: reliability.

plague *v.* — A: to surround. B: harass. C: implore. D: look on the dark side.

battery *n.* — A: forceful protest. B: hodgepodge accumulation. C: group of similar objects. D: encirclement.

renege (rih NIG; rih NEG) *v.* — A: to snub. B: play the maverick. C: take control. D: back out.

fait accompli (feh tah kom PLEE) *n.* — A: sophisticated approach. B: well-planned action. C: finishing touch. D: accomplished fact.

stagflation *n.* — A: controlled prices. B: economic slowdown. C: a disintegrating government. D: cultural dullness.

scuttle *v.* — A: to tease. B: abandon. C: pile up. D: gossip.

procure *v.* — A: to obtain. B: soothe. C: remedy. D: transport.

anomaly (uh NOM uh lee) *n.* — A: unnamed quality. B: likeness. C: response. D: abnormality.

❝Industry is a better horse to ride than genius.**❞**

—WALTER LIPPMANN, USED WITH PERMISSION OF HARVARD UNIVERSITY

> **"** Those who expect to reap the blessings of freedom must undergo the fatigue of supporting it. **"**
>
> —THOMAS PAINE

---

contravention *n.* — A: anarchy. B: deception. C: political gathering.
   D: violation.

feckless *adj.* — A: faithless. B: relaxed. C: ineffective.
   D: without a fault.

pan- — a prefix meaning A: part. B: around. C: all. D: against.

rapport (ra PORE) *n.* — A: detailed account. B: sympathetic relationship. C: period of tension. D: completion.

brassy *adj.* — A: bold. B: hardheaded. C: sensitive.
   D: highly visible.

murky (STAWNCH) *adj.* — A: unclear. B: harsh. C: conspiring.
   D: borderline.

stanch *v.* — A: to reinforce. B: be weak. C: smooth out.
   D: put an end to.

guise *n.* — A: outward appearance. B: superficiality.
   C: normal procedure. D: slyness.

skittish *adj.* — A: amusing. B: jumpy. C: sliding. D: inconclusive.

sui generis (soo ee JEN uhr iss) *adj.* — A: unique. B: suitable.
   C: outdated. D: of one people.

belated *adj.* — A: complaining. B: offhand. C: weak. D: tardy.

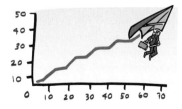

 *ANSWERS*

ethic — A: Standard of behavior; set of moral, personal or cultural values; as, the American work *ethic*. Greek *ethikos* (character).

plague — B: To harass, trouble, vex, torment mentally; as, The company has been *plagued* by a shortage of money. Latin *plaga* (wound; affliction).

battery — C: Group of similar objects used together for a common purpose; as, a *battery* of restrictions. French *battre* (to beat).

renege — D: To back out; not keep one's promise or word; as, If one country *reneges* on an agreement, should the other? Latin *re-* (again) and *negare* (to deny).

fait accompli — D: Accomplished fact; thing already done; as, The plan for joint production of the FSX plane is a *fait accompli*. French.

stagflation — B: An economic slowdown when inflation occurs, unemployment rises and business activity declines.

scuttle — B: To abandon; withdraw from an undertaking; as, to *scuttle* hopes for a multinational pact. Spanish *escotilla* (hatchway).

procure — A: To obtain or bring about by effort or a scheme; as, Equipment was *procured* from local manufacturers. Latin *procurare* (to take care of).

anomaly — D: Abnormality; deviation from the expected; irregularity; as, Cuba's hard-line communism is now an *anomaly*. Greek *anomalia* (inequality).

contravention — D: Violation; opposition; as, The agreement was a *contravention* of free-trade principles. Latin *contra-* (against) and *venire* (to come).

feckless — C: Ineffective; irresponsible; incompetent; as, *feckless* economic policies of the socialists. Scottish *feck* (effect) and English *-less* (without).

pan- — C: A combining prefix meaning all, every, universal; as, *Pan*-American; a *Pan*-European operation. Greek.

rapport — B: Sympathetic relationship; as, growing *rapport* between former enemies. French (harmony, agreement).

brassy — A: Shamelessly bold; insolent; impudent; as, innovative ideas from that *brassy* economist. From English *brass*.

murky — A: Unclear; confused; vague; as, The marketing strategy seems *murky*. Also, dark; gloomy. Middle English *mirky*.

stanch — D: To put an end to; stop a flow of blood or resources; as, America's low savings rate must rise to *stanch* reliance on credit. Middle English *stanchen*.

guise — A: Outward appearance, aspect or manner; as, seeing Hungary in a new *guise*. Also, pretense. French.

skittish — B: Jumpy, easily frightened; unpredictable; as, the *skittish* bond market. Dialectal English.

sui generis — A: Unique; unparalleled; having no equal; as, Due to revolutionary political changes, the economic situation in Eastern Europe is *sui generis*. Latin (of its own kind).

belated — D: Tardy; delayed; coming too late; as, In a *belated* decision, the Germans adopted the policy. English *be-* (completely) and *late*.

Vocabulary Ratings
   9 — 11 correct . . . Good
   12 — 17 correct . . . Excellent
   18 — 20 correct . . . Exceptional

"Be wary of the man who urges an action in which he himself incurs no risk.**"**

—JOAQUIN SETANTI

IMPORTS AND EXPORTS

International trade involves words as well as goods and services. Among our best-known "exports" are expressions like okay, baseball *and* hot dog. *How many of the "import" words that follow do you know? Turn the page for your score.*

tariff *n.* — A: tax. B: payoff. C: warning. D: price increase.

sarong *n.* — A: headband. B: bathing suit. C: loose skirt. D: shawl.

kismet *n.* — A: patience. B: fate. C: resentment. D: love.

nadir (NAY duhr) *n.* — A: faint shadow. B: subtlety. C: lowest point. D: evil spirit.

armada *n.* — A: row of statues. B: cabinet. C: fleet of ships. D: crowd.

Adonis *n.* — A: handsome youth. B: swift runner. C: hero. D: hunter.

sierra (see ER uh) *n.* — A: midday rest. B: place of wealth and opportunity. C: desert. D: mountain range.

facile (FAS 'l) *adj.* — A: careful. B: versatile. C: superficial. D: convincing.

kibitz (KIB its) *v.* — A: to settle in. B: offer advice. C: insult. D: chitchat.

Wunderkind (VUN der kint) *n.* — A: kindly person. B: acrobat. C: film star. D: child prodigy.

66What a wonderful thing is the mail, capable of conveying across continents a warm human handclasp.**99**

—QUOTED BY RANJAN BAKSHI

NATIVE TONGUES

An Irish brogue thick enough to plant shamrocks in.

—Bernie Ward in Sky

A German accent with enough old-world elegance to make even a casual conversation seem bound in fine leather.

—Carlin Romano in Washington Post

---

peccadillo (pek uh DILL oh) *n.* — A: slight fault. B: irritability. C: musical instrument. D: bullfighter's lance.

lampoon *n.* — A: decorative furniture. B: word puzzle. C: unexplained event. D: satire.

chutzpah (HOOTS pah) *n.* — A: concern. B: aloofness. C: shameless audacity. D: inside joke.

debut *n.* — A: conclusion. B: contradiction. C: gracious response. D: first appearance.

Gesundheit (geh ZOONT hite) *n.* — A: "your health." B: "surprise!" C: "bless you." D: "heavens!"

vendetta *n.* — A: dishonesty. B: mall. C: feud. D: meeting.

leitmotif (LITE moh teef) *n.* — A: sadness. B: fantasy. C: recurring theme. D: lighthearted romance.

origami (or uh GAH mee) *n.* — art form involving A: wood. B: fabric. C: paper. D: gardening.

taboo *n.* — A: mystery. B: ancient tale. C: prohibition. D: prank.

smithereens *n.* — A: list. B: broken pieces. C: hodgepodge. D: garments.

66Liberty, when it begins to take root, is a plant of rapid growth.**99**

—GEORGE WASHINGTON

 ANSWERS

tariff — A: Export or import tax or duty levied by a government; as, a conference on trade and *tariffs*. Arabic *ta'rif* (information).

sarong — C: Loose skirt of colored cloth worn by Malaysian men and women. Malay (sheath).

kismet — B: Fate; destiny; as, She looked lovingly into his eyes and said, "Our meeting here must be *kismet*." Arabic *qismah* (portion, lot).

nadir — C: Lowest point; time of deepest depression; as, the *nadir* of despair. Arabic *nazir as-samt* (opposite to the zenith).

armada — C: Fleet of warships or airplanes; as, the international *armada* in the Persian Gulf. Spanish.

Adonis — A: Handsome youth. In Greek mythology a young man loved by Aphrodite, goddess of love and beauty.

sierra — D: Mountain range, especially one having a jagged, sawlike appearance; as, They went hiking in the *Sierra* Nevada. Spanish (saw).

facile — C: Superficial; without depth; as, His too *facile* excuse seemed phony. Also, effortless, dexterous; as, the *facile* fingers of a violinist. French.

kibitz — B: To volunteer advice that is neither sought nor wanted; as, He watched them play cards, annoying everyone with his *kibitzing*. Yiddish.

Wunderkind — D: Child prodigy; young, outstandingly successful person; as, The scientist, a *Wunderkind*, explored the theory of chaos. German (wonder child).

peccadillo — A: Slight or trifling fault; as, her *peccadillo* of talking too long on the telephone. Spanish.

lampoon — D: Satire; whatever humorously exposes foolishness; as, As a controversial public figure, he was the frequent subject of *lampoons*. French, from the refrain of a 17th-century drinking song — *lampons* (let us drink).

chutzpah — C: Shameless audacity; impudence; as, He exhibited amazing *chutzpah*; accused of swindling, he not only denied it but blamed someone else. Yiddish.

debut — D: First public appearance; beginning; as, her *debut* as a concert pianist. French *débuter* (to lead off).

Gesundheit — A: "Your health," used as an expression of good wishes to someone who has just sneezed. German.

vendetta — C: Prolonged, bitter feud with continuing acts of vengeance. Italian (revenge).

leitmotif — C: Recurring theme in music or writing associated with a character or emotion; as, Richard Wagner made extensive use of *leitmotifs* in his music. German.

origami — C: Traditional Japanese art of folding paper to fashion flowers, people, animals and other forms. From *ori* (fold) and *kami* (paper).

taboo — C: Prohibition; sacred ban excluding something from mention or use; as, Certain words or actions in some settings are *taboo*. From the Polynesian language Tongan.

smithereens — B: Small, broken pieces or fragments; as, The vase fell to the floor, breaking into *smithereens*. Irish Gaelic *smidirín*.

Vocabulary Ratings
  9 — 11 correct . . . Good
  12 — 17 correct . . . Excellent
  18 — 20 correct . . . Exceptional

"When goods do not cross borders, soldiers will."

—FRÉDÉRIC BASTIAT

ACCENTS OF INDIA

All of these borrowings from India—the land of Himalayas, maharajas, and Bengal tigers—enliven the English language and weave colorful threads through our familiar talk and writing. How many of these nouns do you know? Turn the page to find out.

atoll (AT ol) — A: arched passageway. B: island of volcanic rock. C: ring-shaped coral island. D: life buoy.

veranda — A: rooftop widow's walk. B: inner courtyard. C: broad view. D: large, mostly open porch.

mogul (MOH gul) — A: traitor. B: powerful or influential person. C: trap. D: man of gigantic stature.

sari (SAH ree) — A: gentle breeze. B: place of refuge. C: hand-pulled cart. D: woman's garment.

mufti (MUFF tee) — A: civilian clothes. B: coarse fiber. C: military uniform. D: hand warmer.

calico — A: bright color. B: fine silk. C: stuffed toy. D: printed cotton cloth.

pagoda — A: garden walkway. B: small wooden bridge. C: temple. D: country palace.

pundit — person who is A: argumentative. B: boring. C: witty. D: learned.

jodhpurs (JAHD purs) — A: running clothes. B: work overalls. C: riding pants. D: turret-like structures.

EXPRESS WAYS

A weaver of tales, he shuttled words back and forth across

the loom of his imagination.

—*Patricia O. Grady*

maharishi (mah ha REE she) — A: dried flower petals. B: prince. C: fish delicacy. D: religious teacher.

cummerbund — A: binding agreement. B: clumsy mistake. C: sash worn at the waist. D: solemn ceremony.

dinghy — A: eccentric person. B: washbasin. C: set of bells. D: small boat.

Brahmin — A: judge. B: elderly wise person. C: aristocrat. D: statesman.

chukker (CHUCK ur) — A: game played with tiles. B: time period in polo. C: fruit relish. D: exercise ball.

nabob — A: wealthy person. B: social worker. C: game played with coins. D: elephant trainer.

nirvana — A: state of peace. B: extreme exhaustion. C: fate. D: hopelessness.

mantra — A: cloak. B: ornament. C: deep-sea fish. D: incantation.

bangle — A: drum. B: temple bell. C: bracelet. D: wind chime.

chit — A: gossip. B: voucher. C: trick. D: tool.

pariah (puh RYE uh) — A: outcast. B: Hindu ruler. C: head of a family. D: canopy.

"Every child comes with the message that God is not yet discouraged of man.**"**

—RABINDRANATH TAGORE

 *ANSWERS*

atoll — C: Ring-shaped coral island and reef enclosing a lagoon. From *atolu*, native word for the Maldive Islands.

veranda — D: Large, roofed and usually open porch, often extending across the front and sides of a house. Hindi *varanda*.

mogul — B: Powerful or influential person. After the 16th- to 18th-century Mongolian conquerors of India.

sari — D: Garment, worn by Hindu women, draped so that one end forms a skirt and the other covers the shoulders or head. Hindi.

mufti — A: Informal clothing worn by off-duty officials; hence, civilian garb. Cloth gown worn by a *mufti* (religious judge) in Moslem countries. From Arabic.

calico — D: Cotton cloth printed with a figured pattern. From Calicut, India, where it was first exported.

pagoda — C: Pyramid-like temple with an odd number of stories, often built over a sacred relic. Sanskrit *bhagavati* (goddess, divinity).

pundit — D: Learned person; one who is supposedly an authority on a subject. Hindi *pandit*.

jodhpurs — C: Riding pants, closely fitted from knee to ankle. From the city of *Jodhpur*, India, where they first became popular.

maharishi — D: Hindu religious teacher. Sanskrit *maharsi* (great sage).

cummerbund — C: Wide sash worn as a waistband by men in India and adapted in Western countries for formal wear with tuxedos. Hindi *kamarband*.

dinghy — D: Any small boat used as a lifeboat or yacht tender. In India, a rowboat. Hindi *dingi*.

Brahmin — C: Aristocrat; highly cultured or intellectually aloof person. In India, a high-caste Hindu.

chukker — B: One of the time periods in polo, a game played by teams on horseback. Hindi *chakkar* from Sanskrit *cakra* (wheel).

nabob — A: Very wealthy, important person. Hindi *nawab* (official under the Mogul empire — from 1526 to 1757 — in India).

nirvana — A: State of transcendental peace. For Hindus and Buddhists, freedom from suffering, desire and earthly attachments, when the soul is absorbed into the Supreme Being. Sanskrit (a blowing out).

mantra — D: Incantation; a sacred phrase chanted or intoned to help one's spiritual concentration. Sanskrit (sacred counsel).

bangle — C: Bracelet worn around the wrist or ankle. Hindi *bangri* (glass bracelet).

chit — B: Voucher for a small sum of money owed to the bearer, as for food. Hindi *chitthi* (letter, note).

pariah — A: Social outcast; despised person. Tamil *paraiyan* (drummer). In India, those who played the drums were members of a low caste.

Vocabulary Ratings

9 — 11 correct . . . Good
12 — 17 correct . . . Excellent
18 — 20 correct . . . Exceptional

SANSKRIT PROVERB

Look to this day
For yesterday is but a dream,
And tomorrow is only a vision,
But today, well lived,
Makes every yesterday a dream of happiness
And every tomorrow a vision of hope.
Look well, therefore, to this day.

IMPROVING WITH AGE

"A soft answer turns away wrath," says the book of Proverbs. And this book of the Bible contains many words of wisdom every bit as pertinent today as when they were first set down nearly three thousand years ago. So, *"get wisdom; get insight"* (4:5). And get your score—on the next page.

diligent *adj.* — A: honest. B: hard-working. C: humorless. D: watchful.

prudence *n.* — A: cautious judgment. B: fussiness. C: morality. D: traditional practice.

devious *adj.* — A: thoughtless. B: laid-back. C: complicated. D: deceitful.

garland *n.* — A: spice. B: wreath. C: ringlet. D: flower garden.

cistern *n.* — A: stream. B: culvert. C: tank. D: tube.

sluggard *n.* — person who is A: foolish. B: pugnacious. C: awkward. D: lazy.

vexation *n.* — A: annoyance. B: slyness. C: unfriendliness. D: fright.

lattice *n.* — A: enclosure. B: covering. C: head decoration. D: shutter.

vapor *n.* — A: breeze. B: ointment. C: mist. D: whimsy.

countenance *n.* — A: reliability. B: facial expression. C: antagonism. D: behavior.

“You can send a message around the world in one-fifth of a second, yet it may take years for it to get from the outside of a man's head to the inside.**”**

—CHARLES F. KETTERING

66 Growing older is not upsetting; being perceived as old is. **99**

—Kenny Rogers

---

repute *n.* — A: reputation. B: gossip. C: denial. D: illicit business.

provocation *n.* — A: solemn statement. B: something that incites.
   C: gloomy prediction. D: inclination.

abhor *v.* — A: to detest. B: refuse to acknowledge.
   C: treat shamefully. D: put an end to.

meddle *v.* — A: to force. B: interfere. C: confuse. D: mix.

importune *v.* — A: to insult. B: convince. C: criticize. D: beg.

crucible *n.* — A: cross. B: piece of jewelry. C: heat-resistant container. D: buttress.

reproof *n.* — A: addition confirmation. B: expression of disapproval. C: silence. D: violent agitation.

envoy *n.* — A: messenger. B: escort. C: royal attendant.
   D: introduction.

surety *n.* — A: equilibrium. B: faithfulness. C: determination.
   D: guarantee.

exalt *v.* — A: to sing. B: boast. C: glorify. D: leap.

---

66 If you have to keep reminding yourself of a thing, perhaps it isn't so. **99**

—Christopher Morley

 *ANSWERS*

diligent — B: Hard-working; painstakingly careful; as, ". . . the soul of the *diligent* is richly supplied" (Proverbs 13:4). Latin *diligere* (to esteem, choose).

prudence — A: Cautious good judgment; as, "... that *prudence* may be given to the simple, knowledge and discretion to the youth" (1:4). Latin *prudentia* (foresight).

devious — D: Deceitful; shifty; as, "He who walks in unrightness fears the Lord, but he who is *devious* in his ways despises him" (14:2). Latin *devius* (off the road).

garland — B: Wreath of flowers used as decoration or as a symbol of honor; as, "[Your father's instruction and mother's teaching] a fair *garland* for your head" (1:9). Old French *garlande*.

cistern — C: Tank for collecting rainwater; as, "Drink water from your own *cistern*" (5:15). Latin *cisterna* (underground reservoir).

sluggard — D: Lazy person; loafer; idler; as, "Go to the ant, O *sluggard*; consider her ways, and be wise" (6:6). Middle English *slogarde*.

vexation — A: Annoyance; irritation; as, "The *vexation* of a fool is known at once, but the prudent man ignores an insult" (12:16). Latin *vexatio*.

lattice — D: Shutter, trellis of crossed strips; as, "For at the window of my house I have looked out through my *lattice*" (7:6). Old French *lattis*.

vapor — C: Mist or fog; as, "The getting of treasures by a lying tongue is a fleeting *vapor* and a snare of death" (21:6). Latin.

countenance — B: Facial expression showing one's feelings; as, "A glad heart makes a cheerful *countenance*" (15:13). Old French *contenance* (conduct).

repute — A: Reputation; as, ". . . do not disclose another's secret; lest he who hears you bring shame upon you, and your ill *repute* have no end" (25:10). Latin *reputare* (to think over).

provocation — B: Something that incites or angers; as, "A stone is heavy, and sand is weighty, but a fool's *provocation* is heavier than both" (27:3). Latin *provocare* (to call forth).

abhor — A: To detest; regard with disgust or horror; as, "He who says to the wicked, 'You are innocent,' will be . . . *abhorred* by nations" (24:24). Latin *abhorrere* (to shrink from).

meddle — B: To interfere needlessly in others' affairs; as, "He who *meddles* in a quarrel not his own is like one who takes a passing dog by the ears" (26:17). Old French *medler* (to mix).

importune — D: To beg with persistent urgency; as, ". . . you have come into your neighbor's power: go, hasten, and *importune* your neighbor" (6:3). Latin *importunus* (unsuitable).

crucible — C: Heat-resistant container in which materials are melted; also, a severe test; as, "The *crucible* is for silver . . . and a man is judged by his praise" (27:21). Medieval Latin *crucibulum* (night lamp).

reproof — B: Expression of disapproval; rebuke; as, "Give heed to my *reproof*" (1:23). Old French *reprouver*.

envoy — A: Messenger; government representative of a diplomatic mission; as, ". . . a faithful *envoy* brings healing" (13:17). Old French (a sending).

surety — D: Guarantee; person responsible for another; as, "Be not one of those who give pledges, who become *surety* for debts" (22:26). Latin *securus* (sure; free from fears).

exalt — C: To glorify; praise; lift up; as, "Righteousness *exalts* a nation" (14:34). Latin *exaltare* (to lift up).

Vocabulary Ratings

>   9 — 11 correct . . . Good
>   12 — 17 correct . . . Excellent
>   18 — 20 correct . . . Exceptional

LEARNING FROM THE PAST

The words in this quiz are chosen from William Safire's widely admired novel Freedom, *about Abraham Lincoln and the American Civil War. How many of these words do you know? Turn the page to find out.*

courier *n.* — A: messenger. B: favor-seeker. C: weapon.
  D: forward-artillery observer.

vigil *n.* — A: lengthy search. B: high-mindedness. C: lighted candle.
  D: period of careful watching.

niggling *adj.* — A: squirming. B: stingy. C: petty. D: straggling.

sedition *n.* — A: withdrawal. B: insurrection.
  C: calming medication. D: libelous statement.

enfilade (en fuh LADE) *n.* — A: raking gunfire. B: long valley.
  C: smoothness. D: sharpness.

baleful *adj.* — A: absurd. B: overflowing. C: kindly. D: menacing.

chary (CHAIR ee) *adj.* — A: kindly. B: smoky. C: confused.
  D: cautious.

purveyor *n.* — A: inspector. B: overseer. C: supplier. D: scoundrel.

summarily *adv.* — A: gruffly. B: promptly. C: thoroughly. D: unfairly.

secede *v.* — A: to replace. B: ignore. C: withdraw. D: win.

lickspittle *n.* — A: fighting spirit. B: greedy person.
  C: good appetite. D: fawning person.

❝Liberty is the only thing you cannot have unless you are willing to give it to others.**❞**

—WILLIAM ALLEN WHITE

66Without libraries what have we? We have no past and no future.**99**

—RAY BRADBURY, QUOTED BY JOHN R. BEYER IN MOJAVE MAGAZINE

---

enumeration *n.* — A: itemization. B: duplication. C: significance.
    D: questionnaire.
reconnoiter (rek uh NOIT er) *v.* — A: to hunt down. B: survey.
    C: reject. D: rearrange.
enormity *n.* — A: foolishness. B: strong desire. C: grandeur.
    D: great wickedness.
celerity *n.* — A: fame. B: intelligence. C: swiftness. D: clarity.
temporize *v.* — A: to plan carefully. B: be indecisive.
    C: tamper with. D: pretend.
bruit *v.* — A: to spread a rumor. B: brood over. C: use dry humor.
    D: suppress by force.
ingrate *n.* — one who A: is ungrateful. B: introspects. C: annoys.
    D: infiltrates.
cozen (KUZ un) *v.* — A: to spoil. B: deceive. C: draw close to.
    D: desire ardently.
caisson *n.* — A: type of gun. B: ammunition vehicle. C: bridge.
    D: gully.

66The reason people blame things on previous generations is that there's only one other choice.**99**

—DOUG LARSON, UNITED FEATURE SYNDICATE

 *ANSWERS*

courier — A: Special messenger, emissary or spy carrying important information; as, "The *courier* . . . had to leave before night." Old French *courrier*.

vigil — D: Period of careful watching; time of prayer during usual hours of sleep; as, Lincoln kept his "*vigil* at the window." Latin *vigilia*.

niggling — C: Petty; fussy; irritating; requiring painstaking work; as, *niggling* money worries, *niggling* details. Related to Norwegian *nigla*.

sedition — B: Insurrection, especially words or actions that incite rebellion against the government; as, He was fearful of being accused of *sedition*. Latin *seditio*.

enfilade — A: Raking gunfire along the length of a line of troops; as, The Yankee *enfilade* created havoc among the outnumbered Confederate soldiers. Old French *enfiler* (to thread on a string).

baleful — D: Menacing; ominous; destructive; as, a *baleful* glance. Old English *bealoful*.

chary — D: Cautious; wary; not giving freely; as, The newspaper editor was *chary* of giving credit. Old English *cearig* (sorrowful).

purveyor — C: Supplier of food or other provisions. Latin *providere* (to provide).

summarily — B: Promptly; without formality or delay; as, "All petitions were dealt with *summarily*." Latin *summatim*.

secede — C: To withdraw formally from a federation, an alliance or the like; as, The South could not *secede* from the Union without a civil war. Latin *secedere* (to go away).

lickspittle — D: Fawning, contemptible person; servile flatterer; as, The general "assumed this *lickspittle* was trying to snatch back his command." *Lick* and *spittle*.

enumeration — A: Itemization; the act of listing; a detailing; as, "The clause appeared in the *enumeration* of the powers of Congress." Latin *enumerare* (to count out).

reconnoiter — B: To survey or search out an enemy's position or situation; as, The general failed to *reconnoiter*. French *reconnaître*.

enormity — D: Great wickedness; outrageous act or crime; as, The man didn't grasp the *enormity* of betraying his comrades in arms. Latin *enormis* (immense).

celerity — C: Swiftness; speed; as, He proceeded to the business at hand with great *celerity*. Latin *celeritas*.

temporize — B: To be indecisive or evasive in order to gain time; to yield temporarily; as, "The government cannot afford to *temporize* with traitors." Middle French *temporiser*.

bruit — A: To spread a rumor; as, "It was *bruited* about . . . that he and his top officers were trading with the enemy." Old French (uproar, noise).

ingrate — A: Ungrateful person; as, " 'Gardner is gone,' Brady continued, 'and his brother, too, the *ingrates*.' " Latin *ingratus* (ungrateful).

cozen — B: To deceive; mislead; trick; cheat; as, They tried to *cozen* Lincoln into accepting their views. Old French *cosson* (horse-trader).

caisson — B: Ammunition vehicle or box carrying artillery shells; as, "He stood on a *caisson* and made a little speech." Also, watertight chamber. Latin *capsa* (box).

Vocabulary Ratings
     9 — 11 correct . . . Good
     12 — 17 correct . . . Excellent
     18 — 20 correct . . . Exceptional

These words are gaining currency or taking on new meanings in the '90s. Some of them, written or spoken daily, are still too new to appear in standard dictionaries. So vault into the future by picking what you think are the right answers. Then turn the page for your score.

channel surf *v.*—A: to sail across rough water. B: switch TV channels. C: sharpen TV images. D: swim between two land formations.

multimedia *n.*—A: information overload. B: combination of media. C: news interpretation. D: TV anchor people.

laptop *n.*—A: piece of furniture. B: tray. C: portable computer. D: small pet.

leverage *v.*—A: to enhance. B: purchase. C: unite. D: compromise.

globalize *v.*—A: to equalize. B: anticipate. C: make worldwide. D: initiate.

biogas *n.*—fuel from A: decaying organic matter. B: natural-gas wells. C: synthetic oil. D: heavy water.

triple-witching hour *n.*—a stock-market period of A: celebration. B: expiration of investment contracts. C: inactivity. D: three price upturns.

megacity *n.*—city that is A: large. B: new. C: ancient. D: abandoned.

transnational *adj.*—A: from coast to coast. B: local switching. C: beyond national boundaries. D: inclusive.

real-time *adj.*—A: as rapidly as needed. B: local. C: unsyncopated. D: broadcast live.

TRAIT MARKS
Optimists are nostalgic about the future
—QUOTED IN *CHICAGO TRIBUNE*
Pessimists always take the cynic route
—ANTONI TABAK IN *THE WALL STREET JOURNAL*

"May you look back on the past
with as much pleasure as you look
forward to the future. **"**

—PAUL DICKSON, TOASTS (DELACORTE)

---

information superhighway *n.*—A: computerized traffic control. B: new school programs. C: space probes. D: computer communications infrastructure.

fusion reaction *n.*—A: detonation. B: meltdown. C: disorder. D: a combining.

on-line *adj.*—A: financially sound. B: pre-release. C: longitudinal. D: connected.

spin doctor *n.*—A: opinion manipulator. B: disc jockey. C: coach. D: forecaster

digital adj.—A: precise. B: clear. C: hand-held. D: using numbers.

aquifer n.—A: air purifier. B: dust particle. C: tree. D: water-bearing rock.

alternative adj.—A: nontraditional. B: mixed. C: suitable. D: lively.

tabloid n.—A: freak. B: sensationalistic newspaper. C: marble slab. D: statistic.

biotechnology n.—study of A: planets. B: brain's evolution. C: human communities. D: modification of products.

Internet n.—A: fabric. B: computer network. C: satellite. D: spy organization.

"Isn't it nice that the new year starts in the dead of winter, when the primitive in each of us believes that we'll never see spring again. Right in mid-gloom, here comes the new year with all its hopefulness untarnished.**"**

— ELIZA G. C. COLLINS, "DEAREST AMANDA..." (HARPER & ROW)

 *ANSWERS*

channel surf—B: To switch from one TV channel to another in search of a more appealing program.

multimedia—B: Combination of modes of communication, such as video, audio and text; as video games using *multimedia*. Latin *multi-* (many) and media.

laptop—C: Portable computer, small enough to be used on one's lap.

leverage—A: To enhance by making maximum use of an asset; as, to *leverage* personal abilities to the limit.

globalize—C: To make worldwide or universal; as, to *globalize* computer technology. Latin *globus* (spherical body, hence the earth).

biogas—A: Gas used as fuel that is a mixture of carbon dioxide and methane from decaying organic matter. Greek *bio-* (life) and gas.

triple-witching hour—B: In stock markets, trading on four Fridays, one each quarter, when three types of contracts expire, sometimes sending markets into wild gyrations.

megacity—A: Very large city; as, *Megacities* of 20 million inhabitants already exist in Asia and Latin America. Greek *mega-* (very large) and city.

transnational—C: Extending beyond the limits, interests or boundaries of a nation; as, *transnational* economic policies. Latin *trans-* (across) and national.

real-time—A: Said of computer calculations: capable of being performed as rapidly as the process or event they describe; as, *Real-time* computing is essential for missile interception.

information superhighway—D: A planned electronic "highway" of 500 channels or more, carrying vast amounts of information and entertainment that will interact with computers and TV sets.

fusion reaction—D: The combining of atomic nuclei to form a more massive nucleus while releasing energy. Latin *fundere* (to melt).

on-line—D: Connected to a computer or telecommunications network; available while so linked; as, *on-line* information services.

spin doctor—A: Adroit manipulator of public opinion who takes damaging situations and turns them into something more favorable; as, The *spin doctors* presented the Senator's blunder as an amusing incident.

digital—D: Using numbers for display or as the basis for electronic information storage; as, a *digital* watch; *digital* recording technology. Latin *digitus* (finger).

aquifer—D: Underground water-bearing layer of porous rock supplying water for streams, wells and the like. Latin *aqua* (water) and *ferre* (to bear, bring, carry).

alternative—A: Designating nontraditional or unconventional choices; as, *alternative* energy sources. Latin *alternare* (to do by turns).

tabloid—B: newspaper relying heavily on sensationalistic headlines and reporting; as, The *tabloids* fueled the scandal.

biotechnology—D: Use of living organisms or processes to modify or make products and to improve plants or animals; as, The *biotechnology* revolution in agriculture will help feed developing nations.

Internet—B: A huge, mostly unregulated complex of university, government and corporate computer networks. Says science writer James Gleick: "No one owns it; no one runs it. It's Everyone's Computers, Connected."

Vocabulary Ratings
- 9 — 11 correct . . . Good
- 12 — 17 correct . . . Excellent
- 18 — 20 correct . . . Exceptional

WIT BIT

Resume: best feats forward—Bob Thaves

Metrognome: city elf—Linda Dimit

IN OTHER WORLDS

The daring and adventure of astronauts in space captivate our imaginations. The words in this quiz come from articles in Reader's Digest *about U.S. space exploits. Choose the answers you think are correct. Turn the page to check your score.*

asteroid *n.* — A: robot. B: space creature. C: tiny planet. D: black hole.

titanic *adj.* — A: unforgettable. B: disastrous. C: ancient. D: gigantic.

composite *n.* — A: solid. B: mock-up. C: compound. D: intricate design.

trajectory *n.* — A: flight path. B: takeoff. C: long-range forecast. D: data.

gantry *n.* — A: entrance. B: movable structure. C: storage area. D: timing device.

orientation *n.* — A: speed. B: quietness. C: position. D: flight schedule.

thermal *adj.* — pertaining to A: daytime. B: night-time. C: barometric pressure. D: heat.

suborbital *adj.* — A: underpowered. B: floating in space. C: without electronics. D: not in orbit.

litany *n.* — A: explanation. B: translation. C: repetition. D: short description.

---

66 The only real voyage of discovery consists not in seeking new landscapes but in having new eyes. 99

—MARCEL PROUST

"The sun, with all those planets revolving around it and dependent on it, can still ripen a bunch of grapes as if it had nothing else in the universe to do.**"**

—GALILEO

---

crescent *adj.* — A: colorful. B: pale. C: shaped in a curve.
D: enfolding.

entrée *n.* — A: access. B: lower atmosphere.
C: sequence of events. D: focus.

refract *v.* — A: to bend. B: back up. C: scatter. D: reconstruct.

corrugated *adj.* — A: confirmed. B: wrinkled. C: sifted.
D: arranged in order.

stark *adj.* — A: brave. B: desolate. C: dangerous. D: unyielding.

dross *n.* — A: reflection. B: filament. C: waste matter. D: spacesuit.

quadrant *n.* — A: escape mechanism. B: fourth of a circle.
C: gyroscope. D: module's antenna.

microbes *n.* — A: pebbles. B: parts of a telescope. C: germs.
D: radio waves.

Perseids *n.* — A: cosmic wind. B: Milky Way. C: moons.
D: shooting stars.

heliopause (HEE lee uh pahz) *n.* — A: solar system's boundary.
B: rocket malfunction. C: absence of helium. D: halo effect.

flyby *n.* — A: aborted mission. B: near miss. C: flight past a predetermined point. D: annoying fluctuation.

"An age is called Dark, not because the light fails to shine, but because people refuse to see it.**"**

—JAMES A. MICHENER, SPACE (RANDOM HOUSE)

 *ANSWERS*

asteroid — C: One of thousands of tiny planets whose orbits lie mainly between Mars and Jupiter. Greek *aster* (star).

titanic — D: Gigantic; of enormous size, power; as, "Jupiter's *titanic* storms." Greek *Titan* (one of a mythological family of giants).

composite — C: Compound; object made up of various separate parts. Latin *componere* (to put together).

trajectory — A: Flight path; as, "They fired Voyager 2's thrusters for a *trajectory* correction." Latin *traicere* (to throw across).

gantry — B: High movable structure with platforms used to service spacecraft. Old French *gantier* (wooden frame).

orientation — C: Position in relation to the points of the compass; as, "Meanwhile, Voyager 2 is maintaining its own *orientation*." Latin *oriens* (direction of the rising sun).

thermal — D: Pertaining to heat; as, "the giant [rocket] booster, groaning and rumbling with *thermal* tension." Greek *therme* (heat).

suborbital — D: Not in orbit; not completing a full orbit around the earth; as, the "historic *suborbital* lob in 1961." Latin *sub-* (under) and *orbis* (circle, wheel).

litany — C: Any repetitive recital; also, a formal prayer; as, "We read through the familiar *litany* of checklists." Greek *litanos* (pleading).

crescent — C: Shaped in a curve like the moon in its first or last quarter; as, "We could see the *crescent* moon through the spacecraft's windows." Old French *creistre* (to increase).

entrée — A: Access; the right to enter or make use of; as, His past experience gave him *entrée* to the Apollo program. French, from *entrer* (to enter).

refract — A: To bend a light ray through mediums of different density, such as air and water; as, "a halo of *refracted* sunlight." Latin *refringere* (to break up).

corrugated — B: Wrinkled; formed into parallel ridges or folds; as, the *corrugated* surface. Latin *corrugare* (to wrinkle).

stark — B: Desolate; bleak; as, "The moon was as *stark* as I'd imagined." Also, utter, complete; as, *stark* terror. Old English *stearc* (strong, severe).

dross — C: Waste matter; scum; as, "These meteors are the *dross* of a great comet that began disintegrating thousands of years ago." Old English *dros* (dregs).

quadrant — B: One of the four equal parts of a circle; as, "Meteors appear in every *quadrant* of the sky." Latin *quadrans*.

microbes — C: Germs; microscopic organisms, such as bacteria that cause disease. Greek *mikros* (small) and *bios* (life).

Perseids — D: Shooting stars; annual shower of meteors mainly visible between the end of July and mid-August, radiating from the constellation Perseus.

heliopause — A: The boundary or fringe that separates our solar system from outer space. Greek *helios* (sun) and English *pause*.

flyby — C: Flight of a spacecraft or aircraft past a planet or other predetermined point; as, "NASA has scheduled asteroid *flybys* for its Galileo probe." U.S. origin.

Vocabulary Ratings

> 9 — 11 correct . . . Good
> 12 — 17 correct . . . Excellent
> 18 — 20 correct . . . Exceptional

IF . . .

". . . those space scientists are so smart, why do they all count backward?**"**

—ORBEN'S CURRENT COMEDY

OVER THE RAINBOW

Color words only describe what we see, and some "colorful" words portray emotions and conditions. How many correct answers can you pick from the following array? Turn the page to see how you rate on this verbal color chart.

verdure (VER jur) *n.* — A: blue. B: fragrance. C: green. D: white.

sallow *adj.* — relating to A: an unhealthy complexion. B: a gaunt look. C: a small valley. D: a facial expression.

rubicund *adj.* — A: countrified. B: jolly. C: moonlike. D: reddish.

towhead *n.* — person with A: an aura. B: light-colored hair. C: a dull wit. D: a golden crown.

cerulean (seh ROO lee un) *adj.* — A: gray and murky. B: shining. C: engraved in wax. D: sky blue.

roseate (ROH zee it) *adj.* — A: ornate. B: delicate. C: thorny. D: optimistic.

hoary (HOR ee) *adj.* — A: rough. B: lewd. C: humorous. D: ancient.

tawny *adj.* — A: spotted. B: brownish-yellow. C: shaggy. D: light purple.

livid *adj.* — A: enraged. B: ominous. C: disfigured. D: confused.

emblazon *v.* — A: to set fire to. B: decorate. C: spread out. D: permit.

iridescent *adj.* — showing A: joy. B: transparency. C: interplay of colors. D: a temporary situation.

❝Our Creator would never have made such lovely days and have given us the deep hearts to enjoy them unless we were meant to be immortal.**❞**

—Nathaniel Hawthorne

TINT TYPES

Jaded by too much luxury

Azured of a bright future —George O. Ludcke

Plum tuckered out —Bonnie Blaser

---

jaundiced *adj.* — A: anxious. B: peculiar. C: sad. D: embittered.

swarthy *adj.* — A: rough and ready. B: hairy. C: pearl gray.
D: dark-complexioned.

tabby *n.* — cat that is A: orange with white stripes. B: black with
white spots. C: light-colored with dark stripes.
D: calico-colored.

hazel *adj.* — A: blue-green. B: gray-blue. C: light golden brown.
D: flecked with blue.

harlequin (HAHR leh kwin) *adj.* — A: pulsating green.
B: yellow-and-black. C: multicolored. D: florescent orange.

terra-cotta (TER uh KOT uh) *adj.* — A: brownish-red. B: rocklike.
C: pale gray. D: tortoise-shell markings.

ebony *n.* — wood that is A: white. B: dark. C: soft. D: pale.

gild *v.* — A: to cover with gold. B: paint in flat colors.
C: make geometric designs. D: speckle.

monochromatic *adj.* — A: glistening. B: dull. C: silver.
D: done in one color.

66Spring is nature's way of saying 'Let's party!'**99**

—ROBIN WILLIAMS

 *ANSWERS*

verdure — C: Green; color of fresh or new vegetation; as, the *verdure* of spring grass. Old French *verd*.

sallow — A: Relating to an unhealthy yellowish complexion; as, The patient was *sallow* and thin. Old English *salu*.

rubicund — D: Reddish; ruddy; as, the cheerful, *rubicund* face of the farmer. Latin *rubicundus*.

towhead — B: Person with very light-colored hair. From English *tow* (fiber of flax) and *head*.

cerulean — D: Sky blue; azure; as, The 18th-century artist Tiepolo is known for the *cerulean* skies in his paintings. Latin *caelum* (sky, heaven).

roseate — D: Highly optimistic; rosy; as, a *roseate* economic forecast. Latin *roseus* (rosy).

hoary — D: Ancient; venerable; time-honored; as, a *hoary* myth. Also, white or gray; as the *hoary*-headed prospector. Old English *har* (gray with age).

tawny — B: Brownish-yellow; similar to the color of tanned leather; as, the *tawny* mane of a lion. Old French *tanner* (to tan).

livid — A: Enraged; angry; as, The insult made him *livid*. Also, black-and-blue; as, a livid mark on the leg. Latin *lividus* (bluish).

emblazon — B: To decorate with bright colors or designs; as, to *emblazon* a poster. Also, to celebrate; as, achievements *emblazoned* in history. English *em-* (into) and *blazon* (shield; coat of arms).

iridescent — C: Showing an interplay of colors resembling a rainbow with shifting hues and patterns; as, an *iridescent* oil slick. Latin *iris* (rainbow).

jaundiced — D: Embittered; resentful; jealous; as, *jaundiced* comments. Latin *galbinus* (greenish-yellowish).

swarthy — D: Dark-complexioned; as, the *swarthy* face of the hunter. Old English *sweart*.

tabby — C: Cat with dark or wavy stripes on a lighter colored fur. Also, a silk or wavy appearance. Arabic *al-'attabiya* (the home of Prince 'Attab where the silk was first made).

hazel — C: Light golden-brown, resembling the hazel nut; as, *hazel* eyes. Middle English *hasel* from Latin *corylus* (hazel shrub).

harlequin — C: Multicolored; colorful; as, a *harlequin* sweater. From a masked comic character dressed in diamond-patterned tights of many colors. Old French *hierlekin* (demon).

terra-cotta — A: Brownish-red, from the clay used in *terra-cotta* pottery, sculpture and the like. Italian (baked earth).

ebony — B: Dark, heavy hardwood of various tropical trees of Asia and Africa. Greek *ebenos*.

gild — A: To cover with a thin layer of gold. Also, to make something seem better than it is; as, to *gild* a mistake. Old English *gyldan*.

monochromatic — D: Done in one color or different shades of one color; as, *monochromatic* paintings. Greek *monos* (single) and *chroma* (color).

Vocabulary Ratings
    9 — 11 correct . . . Good
    12 — 17 correct . . . Excellent
    18 — 20 correct . . . Exceptional

❝People from a planet without flowers would think we must be mad with joy the whole time to have such things about us.**❞**

—IRIS MURDOCH, *A FAIRLY HONOURABLE DEFEAT*
(VIKING PENGUIN)

HEAVEN AND EARTH

Many of our words have their roots both on Earth and in the heavens. How many of these hybrids do you recognize? Turn the page for your score.

jovial *adj.* — A: merry. B: laid-back. C: pleasingly plump. D: ruddy.

pedigree *n.* — A: study of children. B: diploma. C: ancestral line.
D: stamp of approval.

homogeneous (hoh muh JEE nee us) *adj.* — A: relating to humans.
B: similar. C: melancholy. D: cheerful and upbeat.

sleuth *n.* — A: timidity. B: detective. C: carelessness.
D: opening in a dam.

aftermath *n.* — A: result. B: critique. C: concise summary.
D: type of appendix.

cocksure *adj.* — A: cynical. B: angry. C: insensitive and uncaring.
D: overly confident.

nausea *n.* — A: despair. B: uncertainty. C: sickness in the stomach.
D: indifference.

canard (kuh NARD) *n.* — A: ominous warning. B: malicious rumor.
C: humorous proverb. D: small bucket.

ruminate (ROO muh nate) *v.* — A: to become nostalgic.
B: wander about. C: ponder. D: search for.

cordial *adj.* — A: happy. B: perceptive. C: friendly. D: sophisticated.

❝Love beauty; it is the shadow of God
on the universe.**❞**

—GABRIELA MISTRAL, DESOLACÍON (HISPANIC INSTITUTE)

HAIKU

Day slipped the sun in
an envelope of clouds; night
sealed it with a star.

—JOYCE B. ANDREWS

---

reek *v.* — A: to throw into disorder. B: be soaking wet.
C: take revenge. D: give off an unpleasant odor.

solar plexus *n.* — area of the A: abdomen. B: head. C: back.
D: chest.

germinate *v.* — A: to begin to grow. B: be relevant. C: be creative.
D: stimulate.

ferret *v.* — A: to search out. B: camouflage. C: plunder.
D: move quickly.

dog days *n.* — period of A: being carefree. B: having youthful
flings. C: misfortune. D: hot weather.

wheedle *v.* — A: to shout. B: coax. C: pry. D: lie to.

fathom *v.* — A: to understand B: explain. C: decide. D: reach out.

halcyon (HAL see un) *adj.* — A: shimmering. B: pertaining to the
air we breathe. C: fresh and bracing. D: calm and peaceful.

wisp *n.* — A: brief glance. B: hush. C: speech defect.
D: something slight.

oval *adj.* — shaped like A: an apple. B: a banana. C: an egg. D: a
rhomboid.

YAWNING OF A NEW DAY

The darkness came unstuck from the seam where
lake and sky meet.
—LARRY WEINTRAUB IN CHICAGO SUN-TIMES

Dawn crept in tie-dyed majesty through the shadows.
—PETER HATHAWAY CAPSTICK

 *ANSWERS*

jovial — A: Merry; having a playful, hearty good humor. From the planet Jupiter, considered by astrologers to be a happy influence.

pedigree — C: Ancestral line; family tree. Middle French *pié de grue* (crane's foot, which resembles the lines of descent in genealogical charts).

homogeneous — B: Similar; alike; of the same nature; as, Our townspeople are too *homogeneous*; we miss the diverse population of the cities. Greek *homogenes*.

sleuth — B: Detective. Shortened form of sleuthhound, a bloodhound that tracks a trail by scent. Old Norse *sloth* (track, trail).

aftermath — A: Result or consequence; as, The picnic had an unfortunate *aftermath*; we got poison ivy. Also, grass that grows after mowing. Old English *mth* (crop, harvest).

cocksure — D: Overly confident; absolutely certain. From *cock* (rooster, notable for his confident strutting) and *sure*.

nausea — C: A feeling of sickness in the stomach; as, He had *nausea* from the rolling and pitching of the ship. Latin, from Greek *naus* (ship).

canard — B: Malicious rumor; false report. French (duck; hoax). From *vendre un canard à moitié* (to pretend to sell a duck; cheat).

ruminate — C: To ponder; turn over and over in the mind; as, The wise old man *ruminated* on my question. Latin *ruminare* (to chew one's cud as a cow — a ruminant — does).

cordial — C: Friendly; warm and sincere; gracious; as, Her *cordial* welcome made everyone feel at ease. Latin *cor* (heart).

reek — D: To give off an unpleasant odor; as, When accused by a woman of smelling, the incomparable Samuel Johnson is said to have replied, "Nay, madam. You smell. I *reek*." Old English *reocan*.

solar plexus — A: Area of the abdomen having an interlacing of nerves that radiate like rays of the sun. Latin *sol* (sun) and *plexus* (braid; network).

germinate — A: To begin to grow or develop; as, Meetings *germinate* ideas; seeds *germinate* into plants. Latin *germinare* (to sprout).

ferret — A: To search or find out by persistent investigation; as, to *ferret* out facts the way a ferret (a small weasel-like animal) drives rabbits from burrows.

dog days — D: Hot, sultry weather during July and August, so called because Sirius the Dog Star rises and sets with the sun.

wheedle — B: To coax; persuade by flattery; as, The teenager *wheedled* use of the convertible out of his father. Perhaps from German *wedeln* (to wag the tail).

fathom — A: To understand; get to the bottom of; as, She couldn't *fathom* his motive. From *fathom*, a six-foot-long measure of water's depth. Old English *fthm* (outstretched arms).

halcyon — D: Calm, peaceful and idyllic. Greek *alkyon*, a mythological bird that calmed wind and waves during the winter solstice.

wisp — D: Something slight or delicate, such as a streak of smoke or lock of hair; as, a *wisp* of a girl. Middle English.

oval — C: Having the shape of the long cross-section of an egg. Latin *ovum* (egg).

Vocabulary Ratings

9 — 11 correct ... Good

12 — 17 correct ... Excellent

18 — 20 correct ... Exceptional

ONE WORLD

Many words in the news relate to the preservation and restoration of the environment. How many of the following words do you recognize? Turn the page to find out your verbal ecological score.

sediment *n.* — A: particles in a liquid. B: noble feeling. C: cast-off material. D: shallow-rooted organism.

porous *adj.* — A: fragile. B: opaque. C: malleable. D: full of tiny holes.

acid rain *n.* — A: polluted precipitation. B: mist from a geyser. C: vegetation emission. D: nuclear fallout.

jetty *n.* — A: spurt of water. B: conduit. C: breakwater. D: sandy shoal.

sirocco (suh RAHK o) *n.* — A: seasonal South Asian cyclone. B: Pacific hurricane. C: Alpine snowstorm. D: hot African wind.

tundra *n.* — plain in A: South America. B: Africa. C: India. D: arctic regions.

radon (RAY don) *n.* — A: laser beam. B: radioactive gas. C: detection system. D: solar-heat collector.

greenhouse effect *n.* — A: gardening method. B: algae in lakes. C: global warming of earth. D: increased fertility.

estuary *n.* — A: waterfall. B: silt deposit. C: junction of two rivers. D: mouth of a river.

atmospheric inversion *n.* — A: drought condition. B: jet-stream shift. C: reversal of thermal conditions. D: cause of tropical storm.

66The two most powerful warriors are patience and time.**99**

—LEO TOLSTOY

TAKING A BOUGH

Trees playing "London Bridge" with an old country road.

—Marilyn Wolfe

Old trees sticking their knobby toes out of the sidewalk.

—Colleen McCullough

---

spit *n.* — A: outcropping of rock. B: peak. C: point of land. D: fissure.

pristine *adj.* — A: strict. B: exacting. C: unspoiled. D: shimmering.

ozone *n.* — A: engine's exhaust. B: form of oxygen.
C: nature's heat retainer. D: gas in spray cans.

potable *adj.* — A: movable. B: drinkable. C: strong. D: clear.

habitat *n.* — A: native environment. B: outer covering.
C: usual routine. D: historical information.

mutation *n.* — A: a silencing. B: irreparable damage. C: change.
D: disorder.

defoliant *n.* — A: odor suppressant. B: poisonous weed.
C: powerful fungicide. D: leaf-stripping substance.

herbicide *n.* — A: weed killer. B: decorative container.
C: plant blight. D: herb garden.

moraine *n.* — A: crest of hill. B: shallow lake. C: mountain valley.
D: glacial deposit.

toxic *adj.* — A: poisonous. B: long-lasting. C: bad smelling.
D: unsanitary.

66The sky is the daily bread of the eyes.99

—RALPH WALDO EMERSON

 *ANSWERS*

sediment — A: Fine particles of foreign matter in a liquid; as, *sediment* in drinking water. Also, sand, silt or gravel laid down by wind or water. Latin *sedere* (to sit or settle).

porous — D: Full of tiny holes that allow liquid or air to pass through; absorbent; as, *Porous* sandstone stores water. Latin *porus* (an opening).

acid rain — A: Rain or snow polluted with acids released by exhaust from factories and by burning fossil fuels such as coal.

jetty — C: Breakwater, as, a pile of rocks extending into the water from the shore to protect harbors. Old French *jeter* (to throw).

sirocco — D: Hot spring wind from northern Africa that blows across the Mediterranean to southern Europe. Arabic *sharq* (the rising of the sun).

tundra — D: Rolling, treeless plain of the arctic regions. Russian, from Lapp *tundar* (bare hill).

radon — B: Radioactive gas formed from the decay of radium in the earth; as, Homes affected by *radon* can be made safe.

greenhouse effect — C: Global warming of the earth. Carbon dioxide in the atmosphere prevents some of the sun's heat from escaping earth (similar to the way heat is retained in a greenhouse).

estuary — D: Mouth of a river where it mixes with the sea; as, Coastal waters and *estuaries* are in crisis from pollution. Latin *aestus* (tide).

atmospheric inversion — C: Reversal of normal thermal conditions, as occurs when warmer air prevents cooler, denser surface air from rising. Pollutants can become trapped in the cool air.

spit — C: Narrow point of land or shoal projecting into the water. Old English *spitu*.

pristine — C: Unspoiled; pure and untouched; primitive; as, the *pristine* forests of Washington's North Cascades. Latin *pristinus* (former).

ozone — B: Form of oxygen that is created in the upper atmosphere and that protects life from harmful ultraviolet radiation; as, the worldwide *ozone* shield. Greek *ozein* (to smell).

potable — B: Drinkable; suitable for drinking; as, The town's water supply was no longer *potable*. Latin *potare* (to drink).

habitat — A: The native or natural environment of an animal or plant; as, the necessity of preserving vital waterfowl *habitats*. Latin (it inhabits).

mutation — C: Change in form, structure or function in an organism caused by a genetic alteration. Latin *mutare* (to change).

defoliant — D: Substance sprayed on plants to strip growing plants of their leaves. Latin *de-* (away) and *folium* (leaf).

herbicide — A: A chemical that is used to kill weeds, grass or brush. Latin *herba* (herb, grass) and *-cida* (killer of).

moraine — D: Rocks, gravel, sand and clay deposited by a glacier; as, Certain *moraines* may dam streams to form lakes. French, from dialectal *morêna* (mound of earth).

toxic — A: Poisonous; as, a toxic dump. Greek *toxikon* (poison used on arrow tips).

Vocabulary Ratings
    9 — 11 correct . . . Good
    12 — 17 correct . . . Excellent
    18 — 20 correct . . . Exceptional

---

66 The world is so empty if one thinks only of mountains, rivers and cities; but to know someone who thinks and feels with us, and who, though distant is close to us in spirit, this makes the earth for us an inhabited garden. 99

—*GOETHE*

NATURE'S HEALING TOUCH

"We should pay attention to the ways of nature and learn to encourage the body's own innate mechanisms of self-repair," writes Dr. Andrew Weil in the Reader's Digest Family Guide to Natural Medicine. *Words in the following quiz are drawn from this book. Check the answers you believe are correct, then turn the page to check your score.*

aerobic exercise *n.* — activity related to A: meditation.
B: oxygen consumption. C: yoga. D: inflammation control.

prevalent *adj.* — A: infectious. B: widespread. C: self-evident.
D: incurable.

avid *adj.* — A: undisciplined. B: stingy. C: eager. D: belligerent.

succumb *v.* — A: to fail. B: give in. C: continue.
D: keep under control.

botanicals *n.* — A: fossil remnants. B: health foods. C: cosmetic
products. D: medications made from plants.

placebo (pluh SEE boh) *n.* — A: familiar nostrum. B: quiet place.
C: unmedicated substance. D: sleeping pill.

orthodox *adj.* — A: conventional. B: precise. C: rigid. D: skeletal.

homeopathy *n.* — treatment with A: home remedies.
B: small doses of medicine. C: sea water. D: biofeedback.

mandala *n.* — A: historic medical text. B: instrument. C: chant.
D: symbolic design.

holistic medicine *n.* — treatment emphasizing A: relaxation.
B: mind control. C: the whole person. D: holiness.

proponent *n.* — A: advocate. B: opponent. C: interpreter.
D: specialist.

LIKE IT IS

Life expectancy would grow by leaps and bounds if green
vegetables smelled as good as bacon.

—DOUG LARSON, UNITED FEATURE SYNDICATE

AGAINST THE GRAIN
Viewing nature in the raw
Once made me feel ethereal,
But I lost my sense of awe
When it wound up as my cereal.

—MERRY BROWNE

---

antibody *n.* — A: bacterium. B: multivitamin. C: protective protein.
   D: clotting substance.

placate *v.* — A: to pacify. B: compensate. C: be aware of.
   D: conceive of.

itinerant *adj.* — A: occasional. B: sickly. C: traveling. D: temporary.

acupuncture *n.* — medical practice concerned with A: relieving
   pain. B: building muscle strength. C: draining an abscess.
   D: lowering cholesterol.

complement *v.* — A: to flatter. B: make complete. C: duplicate.
   D: enlarge.

therapeutic *adj.* — A: natural. B: curative. C: reinforcing.
   D: energizing.

microcosm *n.* — A: well-ordered system. B: study of microbes.
   C: power of microscopes. D: miniature representation.

tai chi (TY CHEE) *n.* — A: faith and belief. B: life energy. C: massage to music. D: system of exercises.

postulate *v.* — A: to claim. B: question. C: lie. D: be uncritical.

 ANSWERS

aerobic exercise — B: Running, dancing, swimming or other activity that improves the body's oxygen consumption. Greek *aer* (air) and *bios* (life).

prevalent — B: Widespread; commonly occurring; as, "illnesses *prevalent* in an aging population." Latin *praevalere* (to be strong).

avid — C: Eager and enthusiastic; as, "An *avid* experimenter, he began to test remedies on himself." Latin *avere* (to desire).

succumb — B: To give in to an overwhelming desire or force; as, "Why do some people *succumb* and others do not?" Latin *succumbere* (lie down under).

botanicals — D: Medications made from plants; as, Chinese practitioners of herbal medicine use *botanicals*. Greek *botane* (plant).

placebo — C: Unmedicated substance or harmless pill; as, The volunteers were given the experimental drug, while the control group received a *placebo*. Latin (I shall please).

orthodox — A: Holding conventional, conservative or currently accepted beliefs; as, *orthodox* medicine. Greek *orthodoxos* (right opinion).

homeopathy — B: Treatment of disease by medicine given in minute doses that in healthy people normally produce symptoms of that disease. Greek *homöopathie* (likeness of feeling).

mandala — D: Symbolic design in Hinduism or Buddhism that represents the universe or wholeness. Often used in meditation. Sanskrit (circle).

holistic medicine — C: Treatment emphasizing "the whole person — body and mind — as opposed to focusing only on the part of the body where symptoms occur." Greek *holos* (whole).

proponent — A: Advocate; person who supports a cause or makes a proposal; as, "According to *proponents*, [such] training teaches better use of the body." Latin *proponere* (to put forth).

antibody — C: Protective protein in the blood that attempts to immunize the body against specific illness-causing substances; as, Mother's milk contains *antibodies* to protect newborns. Translation of German *Antikörper*.

placate — A: To pacify; appease; as, "Shamanic societies attribute ill-defined illnesses to spirits who must be *placated*." Latin *placare* (to calm).

itinerant — C: Traveling from place to place, usually to do work; as, Andrew Still, a conventionally trained *itinerant* physician, founded osteopathy. Latin *itinerari* (to travel).

acupuncture — A: Method of relieving pain or treating illness by inserting needles in specific parts of the body. Latin *acus* (needle).

complement — B: To make complete; form a whole with another part; as, "Homeopathic medicines may be used to *complement* conventional medical treatment." Latin *complere*.

therapeutic — B: Curative; having healing qualities; as, The doctor outlined a *therapeutic* diet. Greek *therapeuein* (to treat medically).

microcosm — D: Miniature representation of a larger system; as, "The human body is seen as a *microcosm* of the universe." Greek *mikros kosmos* (little world).

tai chi — D: System of physical exercises, developed in China, for self-defense and meditation. Chinese *t'ai chi ch'uan* (extreme limit boxing).

postulate — A: To claim; assume to be true; as, "Another theory *postulates* that the treatment relaxes the body." Latin *postulare* (to demand, assert).

Vocabulary Ratings

9 — 11 correct . . . Good

12 — 17 correct . . . Excellent

18 — 20 correct . . . Exceptional

THOUGHT FOR FOOD

Food labels are changing in look and content due to federal regulations intended for consumer protection. Knowledge of such terms as those listed below can help you shop smarter and eat smarter. Take this test, then turn the page to see if your vocabulary needs enrichment.

organic *adj.* — A: natural. B: synthetic. C: careful. D: toxic.

nutrient *n.* — A: calorie. B: medicine. C: nourishing food. D: mixture.

tofu (TOE foo) *n.* — A: oriental spice. B: flavoring. C: soybean product. D: cooking procedure.

cholesterol *n.* — A: poison. B: fat. C: muscle strength. D: nerves.

vitamin *n.* — A: essential substance. B: mineral. C: digestive aid. D: pep pill.

megadose *n.* — amount or portion that is A: dispensed intermittently. B: large. C: given once. D: generally prescribed.

carbohydrate *n.* — a compound A: produced by plants. B: made artificially. C: high in protein. D: without water.

beta-carotene *n.* — source of A: vitamin A. B: chlorophyll. C: calcium. D: sugar.

ascorbic acid *n.* — A: thiamine. B: bioflavonoid. C: vitamin B-6. D: vitamin C.

metabolism *n.* — A: bacterial growth. B: antibody production. C: homogenization. D: conversion of food into energy.

monosodium glutamate *n.* — A: smart drug. B: preservative. C: flavor intensifier. D: emulsifier.

"Those who think they have not time for bodily exercise will sooner or later have to find time for illness.**"**

—EDWARD STANLEY

SIGNS OF GOOD TASTE
Health-food store: "Get on the bran wagon."
—QUOTED BY R. GIBLIN
Barbecue restaurant: "We will serve no swine before its time."
—MARGARET A. DIERDORFF
Pizza stand: "Another one bites the crust."
—QUOTED BY CHARLENE BLACK

RDA *n.* — acronym for A: Rich Dessert Assessment. B: Related Digestive Abnormality. C: Regional Desalination Allocation. D: Recommended Dietary Allowance.

plaque *n.* — A: swelling. B: weak spot. C: puncture. D: deposit of fat.

serotonin (ser uh TOH nin) *n.* — A: cholesterol-reducing substance. B: chemical. C: artificial sweetener. D: herbal tea.

gustatory *adj.* — pertaining to A: taste. B: overeating. C: sourness. D: spicy food.

amino acids *n.* — A: food preservatives. B: pesticides. C: protein "building blocks." D: cleansing solutions.

fructose *n.* — A: coloring. B: fruit sugar. C: liquid diet. D: soybean milk.

gastronomic *adj.* — having to do with A: stomach acid. B: a medical procedure. C: eating well. D: inexpensive food.

polyunsaturated *adj.* — with fat content that is A: high. B: medium. C: nonexistent. D: low.

sodium chloride *n.* — A: table salt. B: bubbly drink. C: baking soda. D: antacid.

SIZE CRACK
Extra calories we consume quickly become a fat accompli.

—A. H. BERZEN

 *ANSWERS*

organic — A: Natural; as, *Organic* farming doesn't rely on pesticides or artificial fertilizers. Greek *organikos* (bodily organ).

nutrient — C: Nourishing food that sustains plants and animals; as, Broccoli is *nutrient*-packed. Latin *nutrire* (to nourish).

tofu — C: Soybean product (bean curd) that is a good, no-cholesterol source of protein; as, *Tofu* resembles a soft, white, cheeselike food.

cholesterol — B: Fat-related substance necessary for health; as, Too much *cholesterol* is associated with heart disease.

vitamin — A: Organic substance found in many foods and essential for normal functioning of the body; as, *vitamin* B-6 from meats, whole grains, nuts and the like. Coined by Polish biochemist Casimir Funk in 1911.

megadose — B: Large dose of a drug, medicine or vitamin; as, Any *megadose* should be taken only under a physician's supervision. Greek *megas* (great) and English *dose*.

carbohydrate — A: A plant-produced compound — such as sugars (honey or cane), starches (rice, corn, wheat or potatoes) and celluloses (skins of fruits, vegetables).

beta-carotene — A: Substance found in carrots, squash, tomatoes, broccoli and the like, from which the body produces vitamin A.

ascorbic acid — D: Vitamin C, found in citrus fruits and various vegetables. Greek *a-* (not) and Medieval Latin *scorbutus* (scurvy).

metabolism — D: Process by which the body converts food into energy. Greek *metabole* (change).

monosodium glutamate — C: Flavor intensifier, known also as MSG. In some people, it causes an allergic reaction.

RDA — D: Recommended Dietary Allowance; as, The *RDA* of vitamin C for adults 25 and over is 60 milligrams.

plaque — D: Deposit of artery-clogging fat, primarily from excess cholesterol in the blood. Middle Dutch *placken* (to patch).

serotonin — B: Chemical found in the brain and blood that acts as a natural tranquilizer. It is stimulated by eating carbohydrates.

gustatory — A: Pertaining to taste; as, The lasagna proved a *gustatory* delight. Latin *gustare* (to taste).

amino acids — C: Twenty or so organic compounds that are the "building blocks" of protein.

fructose — B: Sugar that occurs naturally in fruit; as, Like sucrose (table sugar), *fructose* supplies empty calories along with sweetening. Latin *fructus* (fruit).

gastronomic — C: Having to do with eating well; as, cuisine planned with *gastronomic* care.

polyunsaturated — D: Describing fats or oils low in saturated fat and not primarily associated with cholesterol formation.

sodium chloride — A: Table salt; as, Doctors may restrict *sodium chloride* intake in heart-disease patients.

Vocabulary Ratings
>   9 — 11 correct . . . Good
>   12 — 17 correct . . . Excellent
>   18 — 20 correct . . . Exceptional

KITCHIONARY

Baste: "finest" in Cajun, as in "Baste damn gumbo ah evah ate!"

Pesto: someone who keeps bothering an Italian chef

Antipasto: people who don't like Italian cooking

Mince: walk around the kitchen in short, rapid steps

—*Quoted by Ray Orrock in The Argus*

As you unwrap the "gift" words below, tuck the new ones into your vocabulary box. They come with a lifetime guarantee of satisfaction, and they can add sparkle and power to the way you think and speak. Turn the page to find your score.

swashbuckling *adj.* — A: daring. B: idealistic. C: drably dressed. D: romantic.

competent *adj.* — A: agreeable. B: inept. C: vigorous. D: capable.

spritz *n.* — A: boat's sail. B: bubble. C: squirt. D: overhanging rock.

omnibus *adj.* — A: threatening. B: all-embracing. C: round and full. D: slow-moving.

ingenuity *n.* — A: innocence. B: cleverness. C: appeal. D: deceitfulness.

canon *n.* — A: barrier. B: noisy gathering. C: guiding principle. D: bishop.

parlance (PAHR luhns) *n.* — A: gossip. B: small family room. C: witticism. D: manner of speaking.

muster *v.* — A: to assemble. B: relieve. C: challenge. D: spread around.

personable *adj.* — A: intimate. B: cheerful. C: attractive. D: superficial.

concave *adj.* — A: curving outward. B: oval-shaped. C: collapsing. D: curving inward.

infatuation *n.* — A: sense of security. B: aversion. C: temporary passion. D: feeling of superiority.

"From what we get, we can make a living; what we give, however, makes a life.**"**

—Arthur Ashe, Days of Grace (Knopf)

---

forfeit (FOR fit) *v.* — A: to exchange. B: give up something.
C: shield from harm. D: pull back.

query (KWER ee) *v.* — A: to question. B: look over thoroughly.
C: follow through. D: act peculiarly.

intergalactic *adj.* — A: extremely fast. B: subatomic. C: radioactive.
D: between star systems.

steadfast *adj.* — A: slow but sure. B: strong. C: friendly.
D: unwavering.

permutation *n.* — A: alteration. B: permission.
C: stable combination. D: seepage.

rookery *n.* — A: gambling spot. B: children's playground.
C: animal breeding place. D: camping area.

ransack *v.* — A: to run wild. B: destroy completely.
C: do things haphazardly. D: search thoroughly.

infamous *adj.* — A: somewhat annoying. B: unknown.
C: simple and unassuming. D: having a bad reputation.

inkling *n.* — A: blemish. B: small object. C: slight indication.
D: assumption.

66Always try to be a little kinder than is necessary.**99**

—JAMES M. BARRIE

 ANSWERS

swashbuckling — A: Recklessly daring; daredevilish; swaggering; as, an old Errol Flynn *swashbuckling* film about pirates. English *swash* (splashing water) and *buckler* (shield).

competent — D: Capable; well-qualified; as, A *competent* mechanic is a blessing. Latin *competere* (to be suitable).

spritz — C: Squirt or spray; as, A quick *spritz* of this or that will not eliminate termites. German *spritzen* (to spray).

omnibus — B: All-embracing; covering many items; as, An *omnibus* bill in Congress includes a number of unrelated items. Latin (for all).

ingenuity — B: Cleverness; inventive skill; resourcefulness; as, the cat's *ingenuity* in opening the refrigerator door. Latin *ingeniosus* (gifted with genius).

canon — C: Guiding principle used as a standard; as, *canons* of good taste. Also, sacred writings of the Bible. Greek *kanon* (measuring rod).

parlance — D: Manner or style of speaking or writing; as, legal *parlance*; my grandmother's quaint *parlance*. Old French *parler* (to speak).

muster — A: To assemble or bring together; summon up; as, to muster troops for inspection; muster courage. Latin *monstrare* (to show).

personable — C: Attractive; having a pleasing manner; as, a *personable* salesclerk. Latin *persona* (person, character).

concave — D: Curving inward; as, the interesting *concave* shape of an antique bottle. Latin *concavus* (hollow).

infatuation — C: Temporary, unreasoning and shallow passion; as, a teenager's *infatuation* with a rock star. Latin *infatuare* (to make foolish).

forfeit — B: To be forced to give up something; to be penalized for wrongdoing. Middle English *forfet* (crime).

query — A: To question; express doubts as to correctness; as, to *query* a company's claim about the benefits of a product. Latin *quaerere* (to ask).

intergalactic — D: Occurring or existing between galaxies; as, *intergalactic* travel in science fiction. Latin *inter-* (between) and English *galactic*, from Greek *galaktikos* (milky; derivation for Milky Way).

steadfast — D: Unwavering; as, a *steadfast* gaze. Also loyal and constant; as, a *steadfast* friend. Old English *stedefaest*.

permutation — A: Alteration or change; complete rearrangement; as, political *permutations* in Eastern Europe. Latin *per-* (through) and *mutare* (to change).

rookery — C: Breeding place of birds, seals or other animals; as, a *rookery* teeming with penguins. English *rook* (black European crow).

ransack — D: To search thoroughly and vigorously; as, to *ransack* a room for a document; also, to plunder. Old Norse *rann* (house) and *-saka* (to search).

infamous — D: Having a bad reputation; notorious; as, No nation can trust that *infamous* dictator. Latin *in* (not) and *fama* (fame).

inkling — C: Slight indication; hint; intimation; as, She had no *inkling* of his true intentions. Middle English *inclen* (to hint).

Vocabulary Ratings
>   9 — 11 correct . . . Good
>   12 — 17 correct . . . Excellent
>   18 — 20 correct . . . Exceptional

❝An informal survey shows that what most people want for Christmas is two more weeks to prepare for it.**❞**

—Bob Stanley in Columbus, Wis., Journal-Republican

JUSTICE SERVED

Sandra Day O'Connor, the first woman to serve on the U.S. Supreme Court, is one of the nation's most influential people. The following words are taken from various articles about her. Select the answers you think are correct, then turn the page for your score.

sheer *adj.* — A: trim. B: strong. C: absolute. D: pointed.

pivotal *adj.* — A: crucial. B: flexible. C: reciprocal. D: ambiguous.

meticulous *adj.* — A: very small. B: tasty. C: interfering. D: careful.

sanctum *n.* — A: approval. B: public square. C: private place.
     D: blessing.

pinnacle *n.* — A: dangerous position. B: achievable goal.
     C: highest point. D: support.

skewer *v.* — A: to spread out. B: pierce. C: misrepresent. D: twist.

whimsy *n.* — A: quaint humor. B: impulse. C: witticism.
     D: moodiness.

precedent *n.* — A: diagram. B: step forward. C: example.
     D: regulation.

overarching *adj.* — A: extremely clever. B: all-encompassing.
     C: theoretical. D: extraneous.

serendipity *n.* — A: nonchalance. B: opportunity. C: praise.
     D: good luck.

equably *adv.* — A: fairly and justly. B: approximately.
     C: understandably. D: calmly.

❝Freedom never yet was given to nations
as a gift, but only as a reward, bravely
earned by one's own exertions.**❞**

—LAJOS KOSSUTH

" Do the best you can in every task, no matter how unimportant it may seem at the time. No one learns more about a problem than the person at the bottom. **"**

—SANDRA DAY O'CONNOR

---

tenuously *adv.* — A: cautiously. B: temporarily. C: insubstantially. D: indecisively.

incremental *adj.* — A: tending to blame. B: regularly increasing. C: temporary. D: powerful.

ramification *n.* — A: problem. B: combination. C: consequence. D: reinforcement.

promulgate v. — A: to start a rumor. B: force upon others. C: punish. D: announce.

confluence *n.* — A: flowing together. B: entanglement. C: clout. D: significance.

stereotyped *adj.* — A: seen in three dimensions. B: picturesque. C: without originality. D: transcribed.

innovative *adj.* — A: daring. B: unusual. C: up-to-date. D: new.

preamble *n.* — A: summing up. B: introductory statement. C: leisurely stroll. D: painstaking analysis.

pragmatic *adj.* — A: practical. B: temporary. C: stubborn. D: rigid.

" Speak not against anyone whose burden you have not weighed yourself. **"**

—MARION BRADLEY, BLACK TRILLIUM (DOUBLEDAY)

 *ANSWERS*

sheer — C: Absolute; downright; utter; as, "her *sheer* physical fortitude." Also, exceedingly thin. Middle English *schere* (free; clear).

pivotal — A: Crucial; vital; on which something turns or depends; as, "Hers was the *pivotal* vote." Old French *pivot* (pin; hinge).

meticulous — D: Extremely careful about details; precise. Latin *meticulosus* (fearful).

sanctum — C: Place that is especially private and reserved; sacred space; as, "She is the first woman to crack the innermost *sanctum* of male power." Latin *sanctus* (holy).

pinnacle — C: Highest point; summit, especially of success. Also, mountain peak; small turret. Latin *pinna* (wing).

skewer — B: To pierce; transfix; as, She *skewers* an attorney who is evasive or unprepared. Perhaps from Old Norse *skifa* (to slice).

whimsy — A: Quaint or fanciful humor; playful expression; as, "Not known for a light touch, she is capable of *whimsy*." Perhaps from Old English *whim-wham* (fanciful object).

precedent — C: Example; legal decision that becomes a model; as, "careful study of *precedent*." Latin *praecedere* (to go before).

overarching — B: All-encompassing; having a broad scope; dominating; as, "a Justice who looks to resolve each case with no *overarching* philosophy."

serendipity — D: The good luck of making fortunate discoveries by accident; as, Her sound decisions come not from *serendipity* but from hard work. Coined by Horace Walpole from a Persian fairy tale, *The Three Princes of Serendip*.

equably — D: Calmly; having an even temper or the characteristic of regularity. Latin *aequare* (to make equal).

tenuously — C: Insubstantially; delicately; flimsily; as, a court *tenuously* balanced between liberal and conservative. Latin *tenuis* (thin).

incremental — B: Regularly increasing; becoming larger periodically. Latin *increscere* (to grow on).

ramification — C: Consequence, outgrowth or result of a particular action; as, Her decision in this case will have important *ramifications*. Latin *ramificare* (to branch out).

promulgate — D: To announce officially or proclaim publicly; as, to *promulgate* policies to safeguard a right. Latin *promulgare*.

confluence — A: A flowing together, especially of streams. Metaphorically, a coming together of people, ideas, events; as, a *confluence* of history, politics and luck. Latin *com* (with) and *fluere* (to flow).

stereotyped — C: Without originality; trite; conventional; as, the *stereotyped* view that only women can be nurses. Greek *stereos* (solid) and *typos* (impression).

innovative — D: Presenting a new way or process; inventive; as, "There has been little *innovative* thinking among courts." Latin *innovare* (to renew).

preamble — B: Introductory or preliminary statement; as, The *preamble* to the U.S. Constitution begins "We the people." Latin *prae* (before) and *ambulare* (to walk).

pragmatic — A: Practical; approaching situations from a realistic point of view. Greek *pragma* (deed).

Vocabulary Ratings
>   9 — 11 correct . . . Good
>   12 — 17 correct . . . Excellent
>   18 — 20 correct . . . Exceptional

" I endeavor to be wise when I cannot be merry, easy when I cannot be glad, content with what cannot be mended and patient when there be no redress. **"**

—ELIZABETH MONTAGU

PUBLIC ADDRESS

*The language of top govern-
ment officials at various
press conferences and public
appearances provides us*

*with this list of test words. How many of them can you correctly
define? Turn the page for the answers.*

agenda *n.* — A: schedule. B: assignment. C: addition.
　　D: common practice.

annex (uh NEKS) *v.* — A: to destroy. B: add to. C: interpret.
　　D: cross out.

defray *v.* — A: to use together. B: pull back. C: provide money for.
　　D: cheat.

dictate *v.* — A: to explain. B: defend. C: understand. D: require.

renegade *adj.* — A: traitorous. B: destitute. C: cowardly.
　　D: uncontrollable.

humanitarian *adj.* — A: patriotic. B: philanthropic. C: common.
　　D: misanthropic.

unwarranted *adj.* — A: nonaggressive. B: unexpected.
　　C: disenchanted. D: not justifiable.

modality *n.* — A: form or pattern. B: transition. C: difficulty. D:
　　experiment.

logistics *n.* — A: new concepts. B: game theory. C: organization of
　　supplies. D: normality.

base *adj.* — A: substantial. B: contemptible. C: reasonable. D:
　　average.

❝When they call the roll in the Senate, the senators do

not know whether to answer 'Present'

or 'Not guilty.'**❞**

—*THEODORE ROOSEVELT*

66Governing a large country is like frying a small fish. You spoil it with too much poking.**99**

—*LAO-TZE*

---

profiteer *v.* — A: to harass. B: make excess profits. C: predict.
D: compete.

implement *v.* — A: to pry open. B: put into effect. C: penetrate.
D: lead or direct.

transitory *adj.* — A: unimportant. B: imperfect. C: temporary.
D: fragile.

flag *v.* — A: to be enthusiastic. B: lose strength. C: punish.
D: challenge.

interdiction *n.* — A: decree forbidding something. B: firmness.
C: accusation of wrongdoing. D: plea for leniency.

format *n.* — A: adherence to standards. B: repetition.
C: explanation. D: structure or arrangement.

extraneous (ek STRAY nee us) *adj.* — A: inconspicuous.
B: noticeable. C: unusual. D: irrelevant.

sequester *v.* — A: to follow. B: round up. C: withdraw.
D: question closely.

mediator (MEED ee ayt uhr) *n.* — person who A: intrudes. B: settles disputes. C: is thoughtful. D: makes demands.

resolute *adj.* — A: determined. B: blunt. C: opinionated. D: cruel.

66All growth, including political growth, is the result of risk-taking.**99**

—*JUDE WANNISKI, QUOTED IN THE WALL STREET JOURNAL*

ANSWERS

agenda — A: Schedule; list of things to do, especially for a meeting; as, an *agenda* for trade negotiations. Latin.

annex — B: To add to; take by force; incorporate the territory of one country, state or municipality into another; as, the town *annexed* the property for a park. Latin *annexus* (joined).

defray — C: To provide money for expenses; as, Contributions from various sources help *defray* the cost of maintaining bridges. Old French *defraier*.

dictate — D: To require; have need of; as, Additional policy-making sessions will be held as circumstances *dictate*. Latin *dictare* (to say repeatedly).

renegade — A: Traitorous; deserting one cause for another; as, A *renegade* group broke up the rally. Latin *renegare* (to deny).

humanitarian — B: Philanthropic; benevolent; concerned with eliminating suffering; as, a *humanitarian* effort to help the homeless. Latin *humanus* (human).

unwarranted — D: Not justifiable; uncalled for; as, *unwarranted* criticism. English *un-* (not) and Old French *garantir* (to guarantee).

modality — A: Form; conformity to a pattern; as, Recent events necessitate new *modalities* in foreign policy. Latin *modus* (manner).

logistics — C: Organization of supplies, transporting troops and the like, for a military operation. Greek *logistikos* (skilled in calculation).

base — B: Contemptible; mean-spirited; dishonorable; as, the *base* treatment of refugees. Latin *bassus* (low).

profiteer — B: To make excess profits, particularly by exploiting a shortage of goods. Latin *proficere* (to gain).

implement — B: To put into effect; accomplish; fulfill; as, to *implement* fully the budget requirements. Latin *implere* (to fill up).

transitory — C: Temporary; existing for a short time only; as, a political alliance that is more than *transitory*. Latin *transire* (to pass).

flag — B: To lose strength or weaken; as, their efforts *flagged*. Perhaps from Old Norse *flakka* (to flutter).

interdiction — A: Decree that forbids or prohibits; as, *interdictions* against free speech. Latin *interdicere* (to stop, outlaw).

format — D: General structure or arrangement; as, The meeting will have an inflexible *format*. Latin *formare* (to shape).

extraneous — D: Irrelevant; not related to or pertinent; as, *extraneous* developments. Latin *extraneus* (external, foreign).

sequester — C: To withdraw; set apart; seize; as, to *sequester* or withhold funds to meet government deficit targets. Also, to seclude; as, the jury was *sequestered* in a hotel. Latin *sequestrare* (to surrender for safekeeping).

mediator — B: Person who tries to bring about an agreement in disputes; as, *Mediators* helped resolve the boundary conflict. Latin *mediare* (to be in the middle).

resolute — A: Showing great determination; steady in purpose; unwavering; as, a *resolute* commitment to saving the environment. Latin *resolvere* (to resolve).

Vocabulary Ratings
>9 — 11 correct . . . Good
>12 — 17 correct . . . Excellent
>18 — 20 correct . . . Exceptional

"When you get to be President, there are the honors, the 21-gun salutes, all those things. You have to remember it isn't for you. It's for the Presidency.**"**

—*Harry Truman quoted by Merle Miller in Plain Speaking (Putnam)*

GOOD WORKS

As First Lady, Barbara Bush won wide-spread admiration for her unpretentiousness, her friendliness and her crusade for literacy. The following words have been used in describing or writing about Mrs. Bush. Choose the answers you believe are correct. Turn the page to check your score.

candid *adj.* — A: quick. B: alert. C: frank. D: protective.

curt *adj.* — A: clear. B: polite. C: prompt. D: abrupt.

self-effacing *adj.* — A: witty. B: unselfish. C: weak. D: humble.

feisty (FYST ee) *adj.* — A: spirited. B: impulsive. C: vicious. D: sturdy.

besiege *v.* — A: to restrict. B: crowd in upon. C: prepare to defend. D: abandon.

quintessential *adj.* — A: urgent. B: exciting. C: ideal. D: especially sensitive.

discomfit *v.* — A: to injure. B: limit. C: smooth. D: upset.

hone *v.* — A: to sharpen. B: whittle. C: lament. D: make a continuous sound.

proprietary (pruh PRY uh ter ee) *adj.* — A: self-centered. B: respectable. C: owned. D: retiring.

osmosis *n.* — A: fullness. B: absorption. C: instability. D: fertile spot in a desert.

recoil *v.* — A: to wind tightly. B: shrink back. C: call to mind. D: strike about wildly.

❝In every community, there is work to be done. In every nation, there are wounds to heal. In every heart, there is the power to do it.**❞**

—Marianne Williamson, A Return to Love (HarperCollins)

---

belie *v.* — A: to stretch out. B: attempt to justify.
C: give a false impression. D: lie in wait for.

disarming *adj.* — A: peaceful. B: shrewd. C: thoughtful.
D: removing suspicions.

misconstrue *v.* — A: to complicate. B: insult. C: misinterpret. D: lie.

telegenic *adj.* — A: attractive on television. B: scientifically
oriented. C: foretelling a future event. D: inherent.

tony *adj.* — A: fashionable. B: gaudy. C: mimicking. D: sentimental.

nascent (NAS'nt, NAY s'nt) *adj.* — A: beginning to exist.
B: with a nasal accent. C: concerning the end. D: prolific.

surrogate *adj.* — pertaining to A: an old-fashioned carriage. B: temporary law. C: a substitute. D: an architectural structure.

traipse *v.* — A: to wander about. B: catch. C: search for.
D: draw up a plan.

diffuse (dih FYOOZ) *v.* — A: to change. B: confuse. C: reduce tension. D: scatter.

ANSWERS

candid — C: Frank; open and sincere; impartial; natural and unposed; as, a tactful but *candid* woman. Latin *candidus* (pure, clear).

curt — D: Abrupt, especially in the sense of being rude; brief; as, to give a *curt* reply. Latin *curtus* (shortened).

self-effacing — D: Humble; modest; keeping oneself in the background. French *effacer* (to rub out).

feisty — A: Spirited; spunky; touchy; as, If provoked, she can become *feisty*. From U.S. dialectal *feist* (a small, bad-tempered dog).

besiege — B: To crowd in upon; persist; lay siege to; as, She never felt *besieged* by circumstances. Middle English *besegen*.

quintessential — C: Ideal; pertaining to the essence of something; as, She is the *quintessential* grandmother. Latin *quinta essentia* (the fifth essence, "ether," ancients believed filled celestial space. The first four: earth, air, fire, water).

discomfit — D: To upset; embarrass; frustrate; as, The interview did not seem to *discomfit* her. Latin *dis-* (away) and *conficere* (to prepare).

hone — A: To sharpen, as a knife; make more effective; as, Mrs. Bush was able to *hone* her public-speaking skills. Old English *han* (stone).

proprietary — C: Owned; having ownership; as, Hers is not a *proprietary* nature. Latin *proprietas*.

osmosis — B: Gradual, effortless absorption; as, to pick up ideas by *osmosis*. Principal meaning: liquid flowing through a porous membrane. Greek *osmos* (impulse).

recoil — B: To shrink back in dislike or fear; as, to *recoil* from such extravagant preparations. Also, the kick from a fired gun. Latin *re-* (back) and *culus* (buttocks).

belie — C: To give a false impression of; as, "Her Secret Service code name — Tranquillity — *belies* the fact that she has several hot buttons." Old English *beleogan*.

disarming — D: Removing suspicions or hostility, as by charm; winning; as, to have a *disarming* honesty. French *désarmer* (to take away arms).

misconstrue — C: To misinterpret; misunderstand; as, Remarks of public figures are sometimes *misconstrued*. Middle English *mis-* (wrongly) and *construen* (interpret).

telegenic — A: Attractive on television; as, Barbara Bush is refreshingly *telegenic*. Greek *tele-* (at a distance) and English *-genic* (produced or caused by).

tony — A: Fashionable; stylish; high-class. Slang, from English *tone* (style, elegance).

nascent — A: Emerging; beginning to exist; starting to develop; as, a nascent *political* concept. Latin *nasci* (to be born).

surrogate — C: Pertaining to a substitute or deputy; as, "They were surrounded by their *surrogate* family." Latin *surrogare* (to substitute).

traipse — A: To wander about; trudge; as, Mrs. Bush dutifully *traipsed* around the world with her husband. Origin uncertain.

diffuse — D: To scatter; spread out; as, She does not want to *diffuse* her interests. Latin *diffundere*.

Vocabulary Ratings
> 9 — 11 correct . . . Good
> 12 — 17 correct . . . Excellent
> 18 — 20 correct . . . Exceptional

66One filled with joy preaches without preaching.**99**

—MOTHER TERESA

POWER TALK

The career of Peggy Noonan, former speech writer for Ronald Reagan and George Bush and author of What I Saw at the Revolution, provides dramatic evidence of the awesome power of words. Ms. Noonan chose the following words as some of her favorites. Turn the page for answers and your score.

hubbub *n.* — A: foolishness. B: center. C: crowd. D: noisy confusion.

temerity (tuh MAIR ih tee) *n.* — A: timidity. B: selfishness. C: recklessness. D: modesty.

incipient *adj.* — A: sly. B: just beginning. C: dull. D: threatening.

demeanor *n.* — A: behavior. B: humility. C: shabbiness. D: fault.

disparate (DIS puhr it) *adj.* — A: frantic. B: dissimilar. C: eccentric. D: scattered.

fractious *adj.* — A: splintered. B: uncertain. C: unruly. D: dishonest.

torpor *n.* — A: ignorance. B: grief. C: swelling. D: sluggish condition.

de rigueur (duh ree GUR) *adj.* — A: forbidden. B: seemingly desirable. C: extremely strenuous. D: required by etiquette.

immutable *adj.* — A: unspeakable. B: exempt. C: unchanging. D: silent.

bland *adj.* — A: mixed. B: not reliable. C: without individuality. D: happy-go-lucky.

"Sincerity and competence is a strong combination. In politics, it's everything.**"**

—PEGGY NOONAN, IN CATHOLIC NEW YORK

OUT ON A LIMERICK
There once was a man of verbosity
Who loved words with savage ferocity;
Waxing profound,
He fell to the ground,
Knocked out by his own pomposity

—M. VENITA VICTORIA

ipso facto *adv.* — A: by that very fact. B: according to what was said. C: contrary to nature. D: by the law itself.

dysfunctional *adj.* — A: unusual. B: efficient. C: quiet. D: impaired.

risibility (riz uh BILL ih tee) *n.* — A: wit. B: humorous awareness. C: off-color joke. D: weak point.

pugilistic (PYOO juh lis tik) *adj.* — A: high-spirited. B: basic. C: confrontational. D: diplomatic.

thrall *n.* — A: slavery. B: fascination. C: disdain. D: hospitality.

propensity *n.* — A: acute mental vision. B: effectiveness. C: sensitivity. D: tendency.

lodestar *n.* — A: good-luck token. B: guiding star. C: burden. D: novelty.

deference *n.* — A: shyness. B: indifference. C: submission. D: rudeness.

angst *n.* — A: annoyance. B: trouble. C: anxiety. D: emptiness.

elegiac (el uh JY uhk) *adj.* — A: classy. B: dignified. C: towering. D: sorrowful.

WORDS TO THE WISE
Words are small shapes in the gorgeous chaos of the world;
shapes that bring the world into focus, corral ideas, hone
thoughts. They paint watercolors of perception.

—DIANE ACKERMAN

 *ANSWERS*

hubbub — D: Noisy confusion; uproar; as, Amid the *hubbub* of seven children, she learned to hold her family's attention. Gaelic *ubub* (exclamation of contempt).

temerity — C: Recklessness due to underrating consequences; as, "Who had the *temerity* to change this speech?" Latin *temeritas*.

incipient — B: Just beginning; in the early stages; as, "young, *incipient* conservatives." Latin *incipere* (to begin).

demeanor — A: Behavior; outward conduct; as, They were assistants with serious *demeanors*. Old French *demener* (to lead).

disparate — B: Dissimilar; utterly different; as, "Freedom — it was the drumbeat that held a *disparate* group together." Latin *disparare* (to separate).

fractious — C: Unruly; hard to manage; as, a *fractious* meeting, with Cabinet members shouting at one another. Also, irritable. Latin *frangere* (to break).

torpor — D: Sluggish condition; lethargic indifference; as, "I was sailing from tedium to apathy with a side trip to *torpor.*" Latin *torpere* (to be numb).

de rigueur — D: Required by etiquette or custom; fashionable; as, Each room contained the *de rigueur* American antiques. French.

immutable — C: Unchanging; as, the *immutable* fact that a President's Administration is influenced by his aides. Latin *immutabilis.*

bland — C: Without individuality or distinctiveness; dull; as, "Then a *bland* young man came into my office." Latin *blandus* (mild).

ipso facto — A: By that very fact; as, Their tendency to disagree meant they were *ipso facto* disloyal. Latin.

dysfunctional — D: Impaired; not working properly; as, "We [the United States] seemed sometimes like a large *dysfunctional* family, bumping into each other in the kitchen." Greek *dys-* (bad) and English *function.*

risibility — B: Humorous awareness; inclination to laugh; as, "His *risibility* was partly the result of a kind of sensitivity." Latin *ridere* (to laugh).

pugilistic — C: Vigorously confrontational; relating to boxing; as, "They wanted a more *pugilistic* approach." Latin *pugnare* (to fight).

thrall — A: Slavery or subjection; enslavement by some power or influence; as, to get out from under the *thrall* of big government. Old English *thrl* (slave).

propensity — D: Tendency or natural inclination; as, their *propensity* for lying and cheating. Latin *propendere* (to be inclined to).

lodestar — B: Guiding star; guiding principle; as, The values of their hard-working parents became their *lodestars*. Middle English *lode* (way, course) and *sterre* (star).

deference — C: Submission or yielding to the opinion or wishes of another; as, His habitual *deference* to others made him seem self-effacing. Also, courteous respect. Old French *deferer* (to yield).

angst — C: Anxiety or dread; as, He was lonely, but not unhappy. He was without *angst*. German.

elegiac — D: Sorrowful, as if from a loss; mournful; sad; as, Her writing has an *elegiac* quality. Greek *elegos* (lament).

Vocabulary Ratings
   9 — 11 correct . . . Good
   12 — 17 correct . . . Excellent
   18 — 20 correct . . . Exceptional

❝Be careful of your thoughts; they may become words at any moment.**❞**

—IARA GASSEN

SPEAKING OUT

Among the most popular radio shows today are call-ins, which provide millions of people the chance to speak out. The following words may help you sound off more clearly and forcefully if you decide to call in yourself. Mark the answers you think are correct, then turn the page to check your score.

sumptuous *adj.* — A: silky. B: lavish. C: light and airy. D: austere.

cascade *n.* — A: cliff. B: mountain ridge. C: waterfall. D: butte.

insatiable (in SAY shuh b'l) *adj.* — A: impossible to satisfy. B: having strong feelings. C: requiring continual effort.
D: immovable.

fetish *n.* — A: sudden notion. B: erratic behavior.
C: feeling of obligation. D: object of obsessive devotion.

penchant (PEN chant) *n.* — A: plan. B: liking for something.
C: decorative banner. D: dreamy thoughtfulness.

explicit *adj.* — A: inflexible. B: knowledgeable. C: clear.
D: intricate.

arcana (ar KANE uh) *n.* — A: remembrances. B: main points.
C: mysteries. D: difficulties.

frippery *n.* — A: wit. B: solemnity. C: trickery. D: showiness.

heinous (HAY nus) adj. — A: wicked. B: beyond understanding.
C: ugly. D: treasonable.

nemesis *n.* — A: accident. B: trusted adviser. C: opponent. D: idol.

❝How much easier it is to be critical than to be correct.**❞**

—BENJAMIN DISRAELI

> **❝**There is always hope when people are forced to listen to both sides.**❞**
>
> —JOHN STUART MILL

---

scurrilous (SKUR ih lus) *adj.* — A: abusive. B: scrubbed and clean. C: lacking swiftness. D: shocking.

mendacious *adj.* — A: tattered. B: outrageous. C: not truthful. D: poor.

vindication *n.* — A: slander. B: justification. C: attack. D: self-righteous pose.

commemorate *v.* — A: to flatter. B: enjoy. C: memorize. D: honor.

meld *v.* — A: to soothe. B: merge. C: purchase. D: glisten.

mordant *adj.* — A: deadly. B: alarming. C: somber. D: sharply sarcastic.

proselytize (PRAHS uh lih tize) *v.* — A: to confront. B: establish. C: be made known. D: try to convert.

duplicity *n.* — A: repetition. B: probity. C: deceit. D: imitation.

hegemony (hih JEM uh nee) *n.* — A: unlawfulness. B: dominance. C: mass migration. D: democracy.

rant *v.* — A: to speak wildly. B: praise inordinately. C: formalize. D: treat with scorn.

> **❝**The cleverly expressed opposite of any generally accepted idea is worth a fortune to somebody.**❞**
>
> —F. SCOTT FITZGERALD

 **ANSWERS**

sumptuous — B: Lavish; costly and luxurious; magnificent; as, an impressively *sumptuous* celebration. Latin *sumptus* (expense).

cascade — C: Waterfall descending over a steep and rocky surface. Also, anything that resembles a waterfall; as, a *cascade* of flowers covering the railing. Italian *cascata*.

insatiable — A: Impossible to satisfy; never getting enough; greedy; as, the leader's *insatiable* drive for power. Latin *insatiabilis*.

fetish — D: An object or activity receiving obsessive or irrational devotion; as, to make a *fetish* of sports. Latin *facticius* (artificial).

penchant — B: Strong liking or inclination for something; as, a *penchant* for politics. Old French *pencher* (to incline).

explicit — C: Clear and precise, leaving no doubt as to meaning; as, The general gave an *explicit* explanation. Latin *ex-* (out) and *plicare* (to fold).

arcana — C: Mysteries; information known only to those involved; as, an attempt to expose a secret society's *arcana*. Latin *arcere* (to shut in).

frippery — D: Pretentious showiness in dress or manners; as, disdain for *frippery* of any kind. Old French *freperie* (old clothes).

heinous — A: Outrageously wicked; abominable; hateful; as, the *heinous* crimes of the dictator's soldiers. Old French *haine* (hatred).

nemesis — C: Opponent or problem one cannot overcome; as, The press became the congressman's *nemesis*. The Greek goddess of vengeance was named *Nemesis*.

scurrilous — A: Abusive and insulting; coarse; vulgar; as, The talk-show host grew tired of the *scurrilous* attacks on him. Latin *scurrilis* (jeering).

mendacious — C: Not truthful; lying or false; as, Voters complained about the *mendacious* statements of party old-timers. Latin *mendax*.

vindication — B: Justification; clearance of blame or guilt; as, the *vindication* of a controversial policy when it turns out to be successful. Latin *vindicare* (to claim).

commemorate — D: To honor or celebrate someone or something; as, Flag Day, June 14, *commemorates* adoption of the U.S. flag in 1777. Latin *commemorare*.

meld — B: To merge, blend or unite; as, His graceful letters *melded* many different people into a political party. Blend of *melt* and *weld*.

mordant — D: Sharply or bitingly sarcastic or cutting; as, the cartoonist's *mordant* observations. Latin *mordere* (to bite).

proselytize — D: To try to convert a person from one belief or faith to another. Greek *proserchesthai* (to approach).

duplicity — C: Deceit; deliberate deceptiveness; as, a broker's *duplicity* in selling phony stocks. Latin *duplex* (twofold).

hegemony — B: Dominance of one state or thing over another; as, Talk shows weaken the *hegemony* of more conventional organs of opinion. Greek *hegemonia* (leadership).

rant — A: To speak wildly or in a loud, extravagant way; as, The agitator *ranted* for hours. Old Dutch *ranten* (to talk foolishly).

Vocabulary Ratings
>9 — 11 correct . . . Good
>12 — 17 correct . . . Excellent
>18 — 20 correct . . . Exceptional

Obnoxious guest replying to hostess's comment: "Me? Argumentative and pretentious? Au contraire!"

—HOEST, KING FEATURES

COSTS OF CIVILIZATION

Alaska's name comes from the Aleut word that means "great land." The selections below reflect the impact civilization has had on Alaska's magnificent wilderness. Turn the page to check your score.

inviolable (in VY uh luh b'l) *adj.* — A: indestructible.
    B: unworkable. C: illegal. D: open to question.
fossilized *adj.* — A: ceramic. B: broken apart. C: fused together.
    D: petrified.
indigenous (in DIJ uh nus) *adj.* — A: needy. B: angry. C: native.
    D: rare.
piscatorial (pis kuh TOR ee uhl) *adj.* — pertaining to A: fishing.
    B: plants. C: tides. D: shoreline formation.
portend *v.* — A: to prevent. B: make believe. C: interpret.
    D: foreshadow.
ecosystem *n.* — A: detoxification process. B: sound location.
    C: functional unit of nature. D: repetitive disposal.
inclement *adj.* — A: unsettled. B: severe. C: mild. D: limp.
inexorably (in EK suhr uh blee) *adv.* — A: relentlessly.
    B: unpardonably. C: maliciously. D: slowly.
irreparable (ih REP ur uh b'l) *adj.* — A: hateful.
    B: unapproachable. C: beyond repair. D: extreme.
remorse *n.* — A: disappointment. B: remembrance. C: regret.
    D: retaliation.

66I think God's going to come down and pull civilization over for speeding.**99**

—Steven Wright

---

migratory *adj.* — A: stalking. B: wild. C: poaching. D: roving.

behemoth (bi HEE muth; BEE uh muth) *n.* — A: seasonal wind. B: stinging insect. C: huge beast. D: underwater reef.

mystique (mih STEEK) *n.* — A: difficult riddle. B: legendary aura. C: unattainable ideal. D: vague feeling.

permafrost *n.* — A: polar cap. B: new glacier. C: frozen subsoil. D: ice floe.

apace *adv.* — A: cautiously. B: patiently. C: haphazardly. D: quickly.

profligacy *n.* — A: wastefulness. B: dryness. C: expansion. D: stinginess.

reclamation *n.* — A: restoration. B: demand. C: proposal. D: seizure.

plankton *n.* — A: age ring in a tree. B: type of fruit. C: minute aquatic organisms. D: exhaust from an engine.

riparian (rih PAIR ee un) *adj.* — relating to A: glacial deposits. B: meadows. C: rocks. D: riverbanks.

seismic (SIZE mik) *adj.* — pertaining to A: rough edges. B: deep valleys. C: enormous size. D: earth tremors.

CITY LIKES

Tokyo's pace is like a VCR on permanent fast-forward.

—Grania Davis

inviolable — A: Indestructible; incapable of being injured or profaned; sacred; as, the *inviolable* wilderness. Latin *in-* (not) and *violare* (to violate).

fossilized — D: Petrified; hardened, especially in reference to remains of a living thing from a previous geologic period; as, examining *fossilized* pollen for evidence of past climates. Latin *fossilis* (dug up).

indigenous — C: Native; characteristic of a region or a country; as, *indigenous* foodstuffs. Latin *indigena* (a native).

piscatorial — A: Pertaining to fish, fishing or fishermen; as, Spreading pollution caused a *piscatorial* disaster. Latin *piscis* (fish).

portend — D: To foreshadow; act as an omen; as, The oil spill *portends* a spirited debate over further exploration. Latin *portendere*.

ecosystem — C: Functional unit of nature formed by the interaction of plants and animals and their total environment. Greek *oikos* (house).

inclement — B: Severe; harsh; stormy; as, Alaska's *inclement* winter weather. Latin *in-* (not) and *clemens* (merciful).

inexorably — A: Relentlessly; unalterably; unyieldingly; as, *Inexorably*, expanding towns encroached upon the wilderness. Latin *in-* (not) and *exorabilis* (persuaded).

irreparable — C: Beyond repair, remedy or restoration; as, to avoid *irreparable* damage to wildlife. Latin *irreparabilis*.

remorse — C: Intense regret for a wrongdoing; as, *remorse* for a moment of carelessness. Latin *re-* (again) and *mordere* (to bite). Metaphorically, one's conscience "bites back."

migratory — D: Roving; especially, moving from one region or climate to another. Latin *migrare* (to change location).

behemoth — C: Huge beast from the Biblical account in Job 40:15-24. Also, anything of enormous size; as, The oil tanker was a *behemoth*. From Hebrew.

mystique — B: Legendary aura of power or mystery; as the *mystique* of the Alaskan wilderness. French.

permafrost — C: The permanently frozen subsoil in arctic or subarctic regions.

apace — D: Quickly; as, to proceed *apace* with protecting the environment. Old French *à pas* (on step).

profligacy — A: Extreme wastefulness or extravagance; as, the dangers of energy *profligacy*. Latin *profligare* (to ruin).

reclamation — A: Restoration to productive use of wastelands or damaged areas. Latin *reclamare* (to cry out against).

plankton — C: Minute, freshwater or saltwater plants and animals used by other aquatic creatures as food; as, Plant *plankton* in the sea produce a chemical that may affect the formation of clouds. Greek *planktos* (wandering).

riparian — D: Of or situated on a riverbank or lake; as, possessing *riparian* fishing rights. Latin *ripa* (riverbank).

seismic — D: Pertaining to earth tremors caused artificially or by quakes; as, Anchorage's *seismic* devastation during the earthquake of '64. Greek *seiein* (to shake).

Vocabulary Ratings
　　　9 — 11 correct . . . Good
　　　12 — 17 correct . . . Excellent
　　　18 — 20 correct . . . Exceptional

❝To discourage littering along Louisiana's waterways, one environmentally conscious group has adopted the slogan: 'Trash is not bayou-degradable.'**❞**

—*Contributed by Marie B. Menville*

FROM HAND TO HAND

You and I are connected, one way or another, with everyone else who occupies Planet Earth. Test your knowledge of interrelationships among people

places, and things. How many of the following words do you know? Turn the page to find your score.

resource *n.* — A: protection. B: urgent claim. C: beginning or origin. D: available supply.

matriarch (MAY tree ark) *n.* — woman who A: has many children. B: rules a family. C: is of noble birth. D: is energetic.

amity *n.* — A: wealth. B: mirth. C: good will. D: a sharing.

catholic *adj.* — A: local. B: energetic. C: devout. D: universal.

familial *adj.* — relating to A: fame. B: comfort. C: food shortages. D: family.

surname *n.* — A: two or more names. B: first name. C: new name. D: family name.

amenable *adj.* — A: capable. B: hopeful. C: cheerful. D: agreeable.

kindred *adj.* — A: variegated. B: related. C: inattentive. D: sensitive.

unilateral *adj.* — A: one-sided. B: alike. C: invalid. D: unanimous.

synergy (SIN ur gee) *n.* — A: state of equilibrium. B: effect of wrongdoing. C: individual effort. D: combined action of separate components.

altruism *n.* — A: introspection. B: hypocrisy. C: unselfishness. D: idealization.

66He who helps early helps twice.**99**

—*TADEUSZ MAZOWIECKI, PRIME MINISTER OF POLAND*

66 Do not commit the error, common among the young,
of assuming that if you cannot save the whole of
mankind you have failed. **99**

—JAN DE HARTOG, THE LAMB'S WAR (HARPER & ROW)

---

reconciliation *n.* — A: re-establishment of friendship. B: diplomatic
maneuvering. C: conversion. D: tactfulness.

spouse *n.* — A: principal heir. B: newlywed. C: guardian. D: husband or wife.

magnanimity (mag nuh NIM uh tee) *n.* — A: hearty enjoyment.
B: great enthusiasm. C: nobility of spirit.
D: soundness of judgment.

nexus *n.* — A: something that naturally follows. B: connection.
C: veto. D: secret intrigue.

consanguineous (con sang GWIN ee us) *adj.* — A: having the same
ancestor. B: insular. C: peaceful. D: fair and just.

fidelity *n.* — A: health. B: playfulness. C: loyalty. D: remoteness.

collegial (kuh LEE gee uhl) *adj.* — relating to A: genealogy.
B: an assembly of diverse pieces. C: friendliness.
D: a group of colleagues.

comity *n.* — A: beauty. B: courtesy. C: wisdom. D: suspicion.

compassion *n.* — A: congeniality. B: spirituality. C: sympathy.
D: intolerance.

---

66 In the coldest February, as in every other month in
every other year, the best thing to hold on to in this
world is each other. **99**

—LINDA ELLERBEE, MOVE ON: ADVENTURES IN THE REAL WORLD (PUTNAM)

 ANSWERS

resource — D: Available supply that can be used as needed; as, to conserve *resources* for future generations. Latin *resurgere* (to rise again).

matriarch — B: Woman who rules or leads her family, tribe or organization. Latin *matri-* (mother) and Greek *archos* (ruler).

amity — C: Good will; friendship; peaceful relationship, especially between nations. Latin *amicus* (friend).

catholic — D: Universal; concerning or including all; as, having *catholic* tastes in literature. Greek *katholikos*.

familial — D: Relating to or characteristic of a family; as, a *familial* trait of becoming entrepreneurs. Latin *familia* (household).

surname — D: Family or last name, as opposed to a first name. French *sur* (over, above) and English *name*.

amenable — D: Agreeable; having an open mind and being willing to listen; as, Both sides were *amenable* to a settlement of the border dispute. Old French *amener* (to lead).

kindred — B: Pertaining to a person's relatives. Also, having a similar nature; as, *kindred* feelings. Middle English *kinreden*.

unilateral — A: One-sided; done by only one or a few people, groups or nations; as, *Unilateral* action may be positive or harmful, depending on circumstances. Latin *unilateralis*.

synergy — D: Combined action of separate components, making the total effect greater than the sum of the individual effects; as, the creative *synergy* of Gilbert and Sullivan musicals. Greek *synergia* (cooperation).

altruism — C: Unselfish concern for the welfare of others; as, the *altruism* of nations that send food to starving people in other lands. Italian *altrui* (of others).

reconciliation — A: Re-establishment of a friendship or relationship; settlement of a dispute. Latin *re-* (again) and *conciliare* (to bring together).

spouse — D: Husband or wife. Latin *sponsus* (betrothed).

magnanimity — C: Nobility of spirit; generosity in overlooking insults or injuries; as, the *magnanimity* of Abraham Lincoln. Latin *magnus* (great) and *animus* (spirit).

nexus — B: Connection, link, bond between individuals of a group or parts of a series; as, the *nexus* between doe and fawn. Latin *nectere* (to bind).

consanguineous — A: Having the same ancestor; related by blood; as, The recent immigrants realized they were *consanguineous*. Latin *con-* (with) and *sanguineus* (of blood).

fidelity — C: Loyalty; as, her *fidelity* to the ideals of democracy. Also, exactness. Latin *fidelis* (faithful).

collegial — D: Relating to a group of colleagues, each of whom has equal authority; as, *Collegial* deliberations can be lengthy, inconclusive and frustrating. Latin *collega* (associate, fellow).

comity — B: Courtesy, especially between nations in recognizing laws and customs; as, the importance of international *comity*. Latin *comis* (polite, kind).

compassion — C: Sympathy. Latin *com-* (together) and *pati* (to suffer). Therefore, a person acting with *compassion* literally shares in the suffering of another; as, *compassionate* emergency rescue-squad volunteers.

Vocabulary Ratings

    9 — 11 correct . . . Good
    12 — 17 correct . . . Excellent
    18 — 20 correct . . . Exceptional

❝We ought to think that we are one of the leaves of a tree, and the tree is all humanity. We cannot live without the others, without the tree.**❞**

—*Pablo Casals*

The appealing or comforting words that follow, if appropriately spoken, may help to improve relationships and negotiations or enhance the quality of life. Turn the page to see how many of your answers are correct.

compatible *adj.* — A: desirable. B: gentle. C: harmonious.
D: likable.

conciliatory *adj.* — A: patient. B: wise. C: careful.
D: accommodating.

facilitate *v.* — A: to pretend. B: congratulate. C: create.
D: make easier.

auspicious *adj.* — A: unlikely. B: trusting. C: free from suspicion.
D: favorable.

veracity *n.* — A: truthfulness. B: eagerness. C: perseverance.
D: outspokenness.

accolade *n.* — A: praise. B: prudent advice. C: celebration.
D: soothing words.

commiserate *v.* — A: to forgive. B: pity. C: tolerate. D: be grateful.

magnanimous *adj.* — A: bighearted. B: wondrous. C: optimistic.
D: unprejudiced.

cordiality *n.* — A: sincere graciousness. B: toast to friendship.
C: deep concern. D: responsiveness.

perspicacious (per spih KAY shus) *adj.* — A: lucid. B: insightful.
C: talkative. D: painstaking.

66Words of comfort, skillfully administered,
are the oldest therapy known to man.**99**

—LOUIS NIZER

> **"**The Bible tells us to love our neighbors, and also to love our enemies; probably because they are generally the same people.**"**
>
> —G. K. CHESTERTON

---

radiant *adj.* — A: spellbinding. B: welcoming. C: humorous.
D: bright and happy.

cosset *v.* — A: to whisper. B: sing softly. C: pamper. D: play games.

incisive *adj.* — A: uncertain. B: hardheaded. C: bitter.
D: penetrating.

largess *n.* — A: thoughtfulness. B: gift. C: good report.
D: great imagination.

beguile *v.* — A: to persuade. B: cause to smile. C: charm.
D: make free from guilt.

meritorious *adj.* — A: well-known. B: extremely learned.
C: deserving praise. D: brave.

ameliorate (uh MEEL yuh rate) *v.* — A: to improve. B: appease.
C: approve. D: ingratiate.

incentive *n.* — A: creative thought. B: stimulus. C: excitement.
D: ambition.

humane *adj.* — A: sentimental. B: kind. C: self-effacing.
D: well-meaning.

tranquil *adj.* — A: modest. B: airy. C: effortless. D: calm.

> **"**The right word may be effective, but no word was ever as effective as a rightly timed pause.**"**
>
> —MARK TWAIN

 *ANSWERS*

compatible — C: Harmonious; working together well; congenial; as, *compatible* partners; *compatible* software. Latin *com-* (with) and *pati* (to suffer).

conciliatory — D: Accommodating; trying to overcome hostility; as, The U.N. Security Council members made *conciliatory* efforts. Latin *conciliare* (to bring together).

facilitate — D: To make easier; help remove impediments; as, to *facilitate* immigration procedures. Latin *facere* (to do).

auspicious — D: Favorable; predicting success; as, an *auspicious* beginning of a negotiation. Latin *auspicium* (prediction based on observing bird flight).

veracity — A: Truthfulness; accuracy; as, The accountant's *veracity* is unquestioned. Latin *veracitas*.

accolade — A: Praise; award; honor; acclaim; as, The teacher deserved the school's *accolade*. Also, a touch with a sword conferring knighthood. French *accoler* (to embrace).

commiserate — B: To pity or express sympathy for another's pain or distress; as, to *commiserate* with earthquake victims. Latin *com-* (with) and *miserari* (to pity).

magnanimous — A: Bighearted; noble; forgiving. Latin *magnus* (great) and *animus* (mind, soul).

cordiality — A: Sincere graciousness and friendliness; as, The elderly gentleman welcomed us with *cordiality*. Latin *cordialis* (of the heart).

perspicacious — B: Having penetrating insight to understand what is hidden or puzzling; shrewd; as, a *perspicacious* judge of character. Latin *perspicere* (to see through).

radiant — D: Bright and happy; expressing joy, love and well-being; as, her *radiant* expression. Latin *radiare* (to radiate).

cosset — C: To pamper; coddle; give special attention to; as, to *cosset* the one you love. Origin uncertain.

incisive — D: Penetrating; sharp; keen; clear and direct; as, an *incisive* explanation. Latin *incidere* (to cut into).

largess — B: A generous gift of favors or money; as, the *largess* given by a foundation for an important cause. French *large* (generous).

beguile — C: To charm, enchant, delight; as, Dr. Seuss's stories *beguile* old and young alike. Also, to slyly deceive. Middle English *bigilen* (to deceive).

meritorious — C: Deserving praise, honor or reward; as, public acclaim for *meritorious* service to his country. Latin *meritorius* (earning money).

ameliorate — A: To improve, or at least make tolerable, unfortunate situations, suggesting partial relief; as, to *ameliorate* the problems of the homeless. Latin *melior* (better).

incentive — B: Stimulus; motivating influence; as, a financial *incentive* to eliminate pollution. Latin *incinere* (to sing).

humane — B: Kind; compassionate; considerate; as, a *humane* nurse. Latin *humanus* (human).

tranquil — D: Calm; quiet; peaceful; as, the *tranquil* presence of the chaplain. Latin *tranquillus*.

Vocabulary Ratings
> 9 — 11 correct . . . Good
> 12 — 17 correct . . . Excellent
> 18 — 20 correct . . . Exceptional

❝Sainthood emerges when you can listen to someone's tale of woe and not respond with a description of your own.**❞**
—ANDREW V. MASON, M.D.

NOT TO BE CONFUSED WITH . . .

People sometimes misunderstand each other because of confusion over a key word or a phrase spoken carelessly or in haste. How many of the following words are you absolutely sure you know? Turn the page to check your score.

lingo *n.* — A: pidgin English. B: enunciation. C: type of dance. D: jargon.

incredulous *adj.* — A: astounding. B: amusing. C: contradictory. D: skeptical.

expound *v.* — A: to release. B: be pompous. C: explain. D: belittle.

magisterial (maj ih STEER ee uhl) *adj.* — A: manipulative. B: controversial. C: cautious. D: authoritative.

abomination *n.* — A: something hateful. B: extreme difficulty. C: curse. D: sense of helplessness.

strident *adj.* — A: hysterical. B: offensively loud. C: ambitious. D: strict and severe.

delve *v.* — A: to muddle. B: put away. C: investigate. D: swoop.

integral (IN teh gruhl) *adj.* — A: essential. B: truthful. C: temporary.   D: logical.

gaggle *n.* — A: surprised stare. B: choking laughter. C: cluster. D: restraint.

ineptitude *n.* — A: unfitness. B: elimination. C: carelessness. D: remoteness.

"People generally quarrel because they cannot argue.**"**

—*G. K. CHESTERTON*

> **"**Nothing can keep an argument going like two persons who aren't sure what they're arguing about.**"**
>
> —O. A. BATTISTA

---

disheveled *adj.* — A: unmanageable. B: deeply upset. C: untidy.
   D: scantily clothed.

factor *v.* — A: to suggest. B: produce. C: calculate. D: change.

broker *v.* — A: to confront. B: negotiate. C: deceive. D: dismiss.

latitude *n.* — A: firmness. B: listlessness. C: lively interest.
   D: room to move.

assiduously (uh SIJ yoo us lee) *adv.* — A: diligently. B: bitterly.
   C: mockingly.   D: excitedly.

snippet *n.* — A: sassy remark. B: small jeweled clasp. C: fragment.
   D: complaint.

civility *n.* — A: legal procedure. B: politeness. C: peacefulness.
   D: loyalty.

conceit *n.* — A: traditional ceremony. B: bold lie. C: generosity.
   D: fanciful idea.

redux *adj.* — A: revived. B: reduced. C: recycled. D: favored.

brawny *adj.* — A: muscular. B: argumentative. C: pushy.
   D: menacing.

GOOD QUESTION!

Is there a difference between a fat chance and a slim chance?

—Robert T. Schwartz

Why can't we just spell it *orderves*?

—Holly Thompson

lingo — D: Jargon or slang of a particular group or field of study, often unfamiliar to others; as, the *lingo* of astronomers. Latin *lingua* (tongue).

incredulous — D: Skeptical; expressing doubt; as, trying to persuade *incredulous* potential customers. Latin *in-* (not) and *credere* (to believe).

expound — C: To explain in detail; clarify; as, The veteran catcher *expounded* at length on how to handle wild pitches. Latin *exponere* (to put forth).

magisterial — D: Authoritative; as, a *magisterial* study of the Civil War. Also, domineering, pompous. Latin *magister* (master).

abomination — A: Something hateful or detestable; as, the *abomination* of genocide. Latin *abominari* (to hate, detest).

strident — B: Offensively loud and insistent; harsh and grating; as, The *strident* manager generated excitement, anger and a brawling brand of baseball. Latin *stridere* (to make a harsh sound).

delve — C: To investigate carefully; research intensively; as, to *delve* into a mysterious cave. Old English *delfan* (to dig).

integral — A: Essential for completeness; as, The program is an *integral* part of his economic plan. Latin *integer* (whole).

gaggle — C: Cluster or group, often disorderly; as, a *gaggle* of questionable gambling companions. Also, a flock of geese. Middle English *gagelen* (to cackle).

ineptitude — A: Unfitness; foolishness; lack of good judgment; as, Arrogance and *ineptitude* led to the team's miserable record last season. Latin *ineptus* (not suitable).

disheveled — C: Untidy in personal appearance; unkempt; as, the bleary-eyed, *disheveled* composer. Old French *descheveler* (to disarrange the hair).

factor — C: To calculate or include as a necessary element in planning; as, The auto manufacturer tries to *factor* in safety, comfort and performance. Latin *facere* (to make or do).

broker — B: To negotiate or arrange in order to influence an outcome; as, He tried to *broker* a new approach to flood-insurance legislation. Old Norman French *broceor*.

latitude — D: Room to move; freedom from restrictions; as, Colleges allow students almost unlimited *latitude* in their personal lives. Also, distance north or south of the equator. Latin *latus* (wide).

assiduously — A: Diligently; persistently; as, He pressed *assiduously* for a simplification of tax instructions. Latin *assidere* (to sit at).

snippet — C: Fragment; scrap; small bit or portion; as, a *snippet* of information. English *snip*.

civility — B: Politeness; courteous behavior; as, the lack of *civility* on many TV talk shows. Latin *civilis* (civil).

conceit — D: Fanciful or clever idea or expression; as, In a nice little *conceit*, the writer was visited by her fictional character. Also, exaggerated self-opinion. Middle English *conceiven* (to conceive).

redux — A: Revived; restored; brought back; as, the Victorian era *redux*. Latin *re-* (again) and *dux* (leader).

brawny — A: Muscular and strong; as, He was the smallest of a *brawny* family. Old English *braedan*.

Vocabulary Ratings

        9 — 11 correct . . . Good
        12 — 17 correct . . . Excellent
        18 — 20 correct . . . Exceptional

"All you need in this life is ignorance and confidence, and then success is sure.**"**

—MARK TWAIN

GETTING TO THE POINT

Short words are like firecrackers with a short fuse: they get to the point quickly. Often they are packed with as much information as their longer-fused relatives. All the words in this test have only one syllable. But watch out—short doesn't mean easy. Turn the page for your results.

taut *adj.* — A: tough. B: tight. C: skimpy and revealing.
   D: believable.

churn *v.* — A: to stir violently. B: back and fill. C: twist and turn.
   D: go in circles.

mesh *v.* — A: to throw together carelessly. B: separate out.
   C: coordinate. D: involve.

boot *v.* — (with computers) A: to shut down. B: eliminate software. C: change programs. D: start up.

squib *n.* — A: young bird. B: small sea animal. C: sudden gush.
   D: short news item.

brood *v.* — A: to worry about. B: treasure or cherish.
   C: cover or spread. D: exact revenge.

grist *n.* — A: dust. B: grief. C: essence. D: grain.

thrum *v.* — A: to play a stringed instrument. B: scan.
   C: rock back and forth. D: smooth over.

rasp *n.* — A: silk cloth. B: cold blast. C: feather. D: harsh sound.

POINTS OF VIEW

I'm trusting. You're naive. He's a fool. —Lori A. Abrams

I'm quiet. You're unassertive. He's a wimp. —Alexandra Frank

I'm sensitive. You're fussy. He's neurotic. —Michele Simos

I'm concerned. You're curious. He's nosy. —Lori A. Abrams

I'm thrifty. You're a bit tight. He's cheap. —Rosemary Proehl

bleak *adj.* — A: harassed. B: plain and simple. C: dreary.
D: quiet and demure.

wane *v.* — A: to grow. B: decrease. C: minimize. D: vanish.

quail *v.* — A: to ease. B: lose courage. C: be humble. D: hide.

zeal *n.* — A: delight. B: frenzy. C: fervor. D: stamina.

bane *n.* — A: act of prohibiting. B: significant document.
C: area or domain. D: cause of misery.

gig *n.* — A: joke. B: mistake. C: lie. D: job.

rime *n.* — A: frost. B: edge. C: salt. D: groove.

fend *v.* — A: to rebuild. B: repel. C: restrain. D: attack.

preen *v.* — A: to elaborate. B: masquerade as. C: dress up.
D: lament.

cairn *n.* — A: ornate vase. B: ghostly presence. C: castle tower.
D: mound of stones.

fell *adj.* — A: fierce. B: extensive. C: slippery. D: heavy.

HOW COLD IS IT?

Cold as a cast-iron commode on the shady side of an iceberg

Cold as a polar bear's pajamas —Larry Wright

Cold! If the thermometer were an inch longer we'd all freeze to death! —Mark Twain

 ANSWERS

taut — B: Tight; as, The plunging steer inadvertently helped the cowboy by keeping the lasso *taut*. Also tense; as *taut* nerves. Middle English *toght*.

churn — A: To stir or agitate violently; as, The raging storm *churned* the sea. Old English *cyrne*.

mesh — C: To coordinate; combine; as, The couple made an effort to *mesh* their careers. Also, to interlock, as with gears. Old English *max* (a net).

boot — D: To start up a computer, loading its memory with the information it needs to function. Derived from *bootstrap*.

squib — D: Short news item, often used as filler material in a publication. Also, a small firework. Origin unknown.

brood — A: To worry about; focus on a subject obsessively and silently; as, Don't *brood* over a missed field goal. Old English *brod* (hatching).

grist — D: Grain to be ground. Figuratively, something used to one's advantage; as, Prison was *grist* for the writer's novels. Old English *grindan* (to grind).

thrum — A: To play a stringed instrument, such as a guitar or banjo, in a monotonous or unskillful manner. Scottish and dialectal English.

rasp — D: Harsh, scraping sound such as that made by a file; as, The sergeant had an annoying *rasp* in his voice. Middle English *raspen* (to scrape together).

bleak — C: Dreary; without hope; as, a *bleak* future. Barren; as, a *bleak* landscape. Cold and cutting; as, *bleak* winter winds. Middle English *bleik* (pale).

wane — B: To decrease; grow gradually less; as, The school's good reputation began to *wane*. Old English *wanian*.

quail — B: To lose courage in the face of difficulty or danger; cower; as, The prisoner did not *quail* before his interrogators. Middle English *quailen* (to give way).

zeal — C: Fervor; intense, tireless and enthusiastic devotion to a cause or goal; as, the premier's *zeal* for a peace agreement. Middle English *zele*.

bane — D: Cause of misery, distress, harm or death; as, Crime is the *bane* of society. Old English *bana*.

gig — D: A short-term job, especially for a jazz musician; as, He played a *gig* last night at a hotel. Slang; origin unknown.

rime — A: Frost; feathery coating of ice formed when supercooled water droplets in fog hit an object that is also below freezing; as, The *rime* on the grass gave the yard a magical beauty. Old English *hrim* (frost).

fend — B: To repel; as, The corporation *fended* off the takeover attempt. Also, to manage, provide; as, The refugees *fended* for themselves. Middle English *fenden* (to defend).

preen — C: To dress up with fussy, painstaking care; as, She *preened* for hours before her date. Also, said of birds, to smooth or clean feathers with the beak. Middle English *preynen* (to prune).

cairn — D: Conical mound of stones set up as a marker; as, A *cairn* stood where the mountain climber had died. Gaelic *carn* (an elevation).

fell — A: Fierce; dreadful; cruel; as, a *fell* civil war. Also, devastatingly complete; as, He lost his house and his job in one *fell* swoop. Middle English *fel*.

Vocabulary Ratings

9 — 11 correct . . . Good

12 — 17 correct . . . Excellent

18 — 20 correct . . . Exceptional

MUTUALLY EXCLUSIVE

Definite maybe —Jon L. Runyan

Real phony—Gloria Schlesna

Strangely familiar—Jacqueline Schiff

 Light heavyweight—C. P. Miscavish

THE LONG AND SHORT

"The long and short" of this test—the sum and substance—is that half of the words are long and half have only one syllable. How many of these words to you know? Choose your answers; then turn the page to find your score.

bray *n.* — A: donkey cry. B: rough edge. C: barrier. D: woven ornamental trimming.

ambulatory *adj.* — A: without direction. B: seriously injured. C: able to walk. D: energetic.

broach *v.* — A: to introduce or mention. B: connect with. C: disagree with. D: shock.

deferential *adj.* — A: shy. B: without interest. C: mechanical. D: respectful.

née (NAY) *adj.* — relating to A: place. B: birth name. C: size. D: attitude.

manifestation *n.* — A: encounter. B: indication. C: strong inclination. D: fullness.

snide *adj.* — A: clever. B: malicious. C: abrupt. D: whispered.

heterogeneous (het ur uh JEE nee us) *adj.* — A: confusing. B: talented. C: congenial. D: varied.

lee *n.* — A: forefront. B: edge. C: shelter. D: bottom.

cartographer (car TOG ruh fer) *n.* — A: disposal engineer. B: heart specialist. C: astronomer. D: map-maker.

orb *n.* — A: piece of jewelry. B: historical find. C: computer term. D: globe.

❝Discipline is remembering what you want.❞

—DAVID CAMPBELL

WIT BITS

Cheese grater: cheddar shredder —John Wood

Sore loser: bitter quitter —John Dratwa

Earthquake: chasm spasm —Ellis Stewart

---

intransigent (in TRAN suh jent) *adj.* — A: practical.
   B: uncompromising. C: not lasting. D: clairvoyant.

scam *n.* — A: swindle. B: outline. C: superficial examination.
   D: quick getaway.

extemporaneous (ek stem puh RAY nee us) *adj.* — A: timeless.
   B: haphazard. C: unrehearsed. D: rapid.

wry *adj.* — pertaining to A: meditative thought. B: sweet memory.
   C: facial expression. D: pain.

misapprehension *n.* — A: lack of fear. B: worry. C: unfair seizure.
   D: misunderstanding.

niche *n.* — A: cupboard. B: recess in a wall. C: noticeable scratch.
   D: interlocking part.

disingenuous (dis in JEN you us) *adj.* — A: uncaring. B: clumsy.
   C: innocent. D: insincere.

splotch *n.* — A: small quantity. B: stain or spot.
   C: irregular pattern. D: descriptive sound.

blasphemous (BLAS fuh mus) *adj.* — A: slanderous. B: profane.
   C: angry. D: volatile.

**❝To have a right to do a thing is not at all the same
as to be right in doing it.❞**

—*G. K. CHESTERTON*

 *ANSWERS*

bray — A: Loud, harsh cry, as from a donkey. Old French *braire* (to cry out).

ambulatory — C: Able to walk about; as, an *ambulatory* patient. Also, pertaining to walking; as, *ambulatory* exercise. Latin *ambulare* (to walk).

broach — A: To introduce or mention a topic for discussion. Also, to tap or pierce a keg. Latin *broccus* (projecting).

deferential — D: Respectful; yielding to someone else's wishes or judgment; as, the student's *deferential* attitude toward his teacher. Latin *deferre* (to carry down).

née — B: Born; referring to the maiden name of a married woman; as, Mrs. Mary Lincoln, *n*[acute]*ée* Todd. French, from *na*[cir]*ître* (to be born).

manifestation — B: Indication or evidence of the nature of a person or thing; as, The mechanic's repair was a *manifestation* of his skill. Latin *manifestus* (evident).

snide — B: Malicious; nasty; spiteful; as, The *snide* comment hurt her. Origin uncertain.

heterogeneous — D: Varied; consisting of unlike people or things; as, Most political parties are composed of *heterogeneous* personalities. Greek *hetero-* (other) and *genos* (kind, gender).

lee — C: Shelter or protection, especially from a storm; as, to crouch in the *lee* of a rock during a squall. Old English *hleo* (shelter).

cartographer — D: Someone who makes maps. French *carte* (map) and Greek *-graphia* (writing).

orb — D: Globe or sphere; as, the bright *orb* of the street lamp. Also, poetic description of a heavenly body. Latin *orbis* (circle).

intransigent — B: Uncompromising; stubbornly refusing to give up an outlook or position; as, The committee's *intransigent* policy created problems. Latin *in-* (not) and *transigere* (to agree).

scam — A: Swindle; dishonest scheme to make a quick profit; as, the horse-racing *scam* in the film *The Sting*. American slang; origin uncertain.

extemporaneous —C: Unrehearsed; offhand; as, an *extemporaneous* speech. Latin *ex tempore* (at the moment).

wry — C: Pertaining to anything twisted or distorted, especially a facial expression indicating displeasure or disgust; as, a *wry* smile. Also, ironic, perverse or mocking; as, *wry* humor. Old English *wrigian* (to turn).

misapprehension — D: Misunderstanding; mistaken idea; as, a *misapprehension* in negotiations between labor and management. English *mis-* (wrongly) and Latin *apprehendere* (to grasp).

niche — B: Recess in a wall for displaying an object. Also, figuratively, a position suitable for a person; as, She found her *niche* as a counselor. French.

disingenuous — D: Insincere; deceitful; not straightforward; as, a *disingenuous* witness. Latin *dis-* (away from) and *ingenuus* (noble).

splotch — B: Stain; spot; as, an ugly *splotch* on the rug. Possibly a blend of *spot* and *blotch*.

blasphemous — B: Profane; showing disrespect for God or anything held sacred or in high esteem; as, a *blasphemous* book. Greek *blasphemos* (speaking evil).

Vocabulary Ratings
> 9 — 11 correct . . . Good
> 12 — 17 correct . . . Excellent
> 18 — 20 correct . . . Exceptional

❝An invasion of armies can be resisted, but not an idea whose time has come.**❞**

—Victor Hugo

COLORFULLY COMMONPLACE

In your everyday vocabulary you have a variety of interesting words at hand that range from the commonplace to the color-fully technical. Mark the answer you think is correct and turn the page for your score.

swatch *n.* — A: a quick blow. B: petty theft. C: sample of cloth. D: repair of clothing.

linchpin *n.* — A: lapel jewelry. B: start-up computer switch. C: release mechanism. D: part of an axle.

console *n.* — A: support group. B: security blanket. C: marriage partner. D: cabinet.

coiffure (kwa FYOOR) *n.* — A: dress designer. B: hair style. C: silver service. D: curved railing.

ultraviolet *adj.* — having A: short, invisible wavelengths. B: a bluish pigment. C: visible, long wavelengths. D: a deep-purple color.

distaff *adj.* — relating to A: helpers. B: women. C: distance. D: melancholy.

hidebound *adj.* — A: tactless. B: leather-covered. C: tough. D: inflexible.

taproot *n.* — A: main plant root. B: engineering structure. C: dance with metal-tipped shoes. D: solution to a problem.

manger (MAIN jur) *n.* — A: feed box. B: bunk bed. C: dwelling. D: mattress.

highboy *n.* — A: chest of drawers. B: swindler. C: snob. D: chair for babies.

GOOD QUESTION!

Why is there a permanent press setting on most irons?

—Kay Mosure

How do you know when you've run out of invisible ink?

—Larry Andersen

❝No wonder kids today can't spell. They're surrounded by signs like: 'Suzi's All-Nite E-Z Drive-Thru Donut Shoppe.'**❞**

—DAVE BARRY IN TROPIC MAGAZINE

condiment *n.* — A: candy. B: seasoning. C: combination.
   D: channel.
winnow *v.* — A: to succeed. B: coax. C: separate. D: shrink from.
flange *n.* — A: hanging shelf. B: wedge. C: long, thin object.
   D: projecting rim or edge.
hutch *n.* — A: lake eel. B: toolshed. C: window seat.
   D: pen for small animals.
trappings *n.* — A: sly tricks. B: accommodations.
   C: ornamental accessories. D: loose floorboards.
napery *n.* — A: soft, downy surface. B: Japanese sleeping mat.
   C: household linen. D: place of quiet.
aerate (AIR ate) *v.* — A: to lighten. B: expose to air. C: puff out.
   D: bring to public notice.
impeller *n.* — A: rotor blade. B: barrier. C: wrench. D: amplifier.
cloche (KLOHSH) *n.* — A: hose attachment. B: sundial.
   C: type of divider. D: bell-shaped cover.
fusion *n.* — A: a splitting apart. B: jumble or muddle. C: blending.
   D: warmth of feeling.

 ANSWERS

swatch — C: Sample of cloth; patch or characteristic specimen; as, to take home *swatches* of rugs for color selection. Origin unknown.

linchpin — D: Axle pin that keeps a wheel in place; essential person or thing. Old English *lynis*.

console — D: Cabinet for radio, television, record player. Also, an ornamental bracket. French, from *consolateur* (a bracket in the shape of a carved figure).

coiffure — B: Style of hair arrangement; as, a *coiffure* of loose curls. Also, a headdress. French *coiffe* (cap).

ultraviolet — A: Having short wavelengths beyond the visible spectrum at the violet end; as, Sunlight's *ultraviolet* rays increase the risk of skin cancer. Latin *ultra-* (beyond) and English *violet*.

distaff—B: Relating to women or to maternal lineage; as, the *distaff* side of the President's family. Old English *distæf* (a mechanism to hold wool for spinning).

hidebound—D: Inflexible and narrow-minded; locked into old customs and prejudices; as, a *hidebound* official. From the tightly stretched skin on starving cattle.

taproot—A: Main, vertical root from which others branch out. Metaphorically, anything that serves as a primary source of strength; as, Freedom of speech is the *taproot* of American democracy. Old English *tæappa* (tap).

manger—A: Feed box for livestock; as, In the stable "she . . . laid him in a *manger* because there was no room for them in the inn." Old French *mangier* (to eat).

highboy—A: tall chest of drawers on legs.

condiment—B: A seasoning or sauce, such as pepper and mustard, that adds special flavor to food. Latin *condire* (to season).

winnow—C: To separate; sift the good from the bad; as, to *winnow* facts from rumors. Also, to throw grain into the breeze so that lighter chaff (husks) and dirt will blow away. Old English *windwian* (to fan).

flange—D: Projecting rim or edge, as on some window screens to hold them in place. Old French *flanche* (flank, side).

hutch—D: Pen or coop for small animals; also, a cupboard with open shelves on top to display objects. Old French *huche*.

trappings—C: Ornamental accessories; outward signs or indications. Old French *drap* (cloth).

napery—C: Household linen, such as napkins and tablecloths. Old French *nappe*.

aerate—B: To expose to air or cause air to circulate through; as, to *aerate* a reservoir's water supply by using fountains. Greek *aer* (air).

impeller—A: Rotor blade; device used to force a liquid along a pipe or move it within a closed area; as, a dishwasher's *impeller*. Latin *impellere* (to drive).

cloche—D: Bell-shaped glass cover for plants, food, and the like. Also, closefitting woman's hat of the 1920s. French (bell).

fusion—C: A blending together; as, an athlete's *fusion* of speed and skill; also, the combining of two light nuclei to form a heavier nucleus with a loss of mass, which is converted into energy. Latin *fundere* (to melt).

Vocabulary Ratings
> 9 — 11 correct . . . Good
> 12 — 17 correct . . . Excellent
> 18 — 20 correct . . . Exceptional

---

66 I like trees because they seem more resigned to the way they have to live than other things do. **99**
—WILLA CATHER

MORE THAN MEETS THE EYE

Look-alikes can cause mistaken-identity problems among words as well as people. In this test you may find yourself hesitating over the meanings of the following paired words before finding the best answers. Turn the page to find out how you did.

affect v. — A: to influence. B: plan. C: conclude. D: undertake.

effect v. — A: to be the cause of. B: preclude. C: think up.
D: adjust or control.

illicit adj. — A: provocative. B: unlawful. C: secret. D: abnormal.

elicit v. — A: to demand. B: evoke. C: break the law. D: ask for.

perimeter (puh RIM uh tur) n. — A: proportion. B: territory.
C: outer boundary. D: parade ground.

parameter (puh RAM uh tur) n. — A: simultaneous occurrence.
B: periphery. C: mathematical quantity. D: substitute.

classical adj. — A: modern. B: outdated. C: remarkable.
D: of Greek and Roman culture.

classic adj. — A: up-to-date. B: timely. C: of the highest quality.
D: old-fashioned.

evanescent adj. — A: sparkling. B: fading quickly. C: colorful.
D: flashing on and off.

effervescent adj. — A: bubbling. B: crystal clear. C: momentary.
D: lacking charisma.

MODIFIED MAXIMS

An ounce of pretension is worth a pound of manure.

—MARTHA SIMMONS

Caveman's motto: He who hesitates is lunch.

—STEPHEN C. LEAHY

Jockey's rule of thumb: Put your money where your mount is.

—PHYLLIS JEAN PORTER

> **"**What counts is not necessarily the size of the dog in the fight—it's the size of the fight in the dog.**"**
>
> —DWIGHT D. EISENHOWER

---

voracious *adj.* — A: vicious. B: exciting. C: insatiable. D: truthful.

rapacious *adj.* — A: evil. B: frightening. C: famished. D: greedy.

judicious *adj.* — A: diplomatic. B: wise. C: watchful. D: legal.

judicial *adj.* — A: ponderous. B: unbiased. C: sudden. D: prudent.

cynical *adj.* — A: ill-tempered. B: disguising feelings.
C: contemptuously distrustful. D: reluctant to perform.

skeptical *adj.* — A: dissenting. B: bigoted. C: heckling.
D: unconvinced.

obtuse *adj.* — A: complicated. B: unreasonable. C: angular. D: dull.

abstruse *adj.* — A: difficult to understand. B: unintelligent.
C: strangely different. D: straightforward.

queue *n.* — A: oval design. B: line of people. C: theory.
D: indication.

cue *n.* — A: indoor game. B: orderly formation.
C: guiding suggestion. D: solution.

INCREDIBLE EDIBLES

Bakery: "Cakes 66¢—Upside-down cakes 99¢"

—SHARON FLYNN

Fish Market: "Lox, stocked in barrel"

—BRIAN S. HALL

affect — A: To influence; produce a response; as, People are deeply *affected* by Picasso's anti-war painting "Guernica." Latin *afficere*.

effect — A: To be the cause of; bring about; as, to *effect* the unification of the two Germanys. Latin *efficere*.

illicit — B: Unlawful; unauthorized; as, Stock-exchange rules prohibit *illicit* trading in securities. Latin *illicitus*.

elicit — B: To evoke a response or reaction; draw out; as, The inquiry *elicited* important facts. Latin *elicere*.

perimeter — C: Outer boundary; as, We walked the *perimeter* of our farm. Greek *peri-* (around) and *metron* (measure).

parameter — C: Varying mathematical quantity whose values determine a system's form; as, death and survival *parameters* from insurance statistics. Informally, a guide; as, foreign-policy *parameters*. Latin *para-* (beside) and *metron*.

classical — D: Of Greek and Roman culture; as, a *classical* scholar. Also, traditional, as classical architecture or music. Latin *classicus* (superior).

classic — C: Of the highest quality; serving as a standard; as, Melville's *Moby Dick* is a *classic* American novel. Latin *classicus*.

evanescent — B: Fading quickly; barely perceptible; as, an *evanescent* dream. Latin *evanescere* (to vanish).

effervescent — A: Bubbling; as, an *effervescent* soft drink. Also, vivacious; as, an *effervescent* personality. Latin *effervescere* (to boil over).

voracious — C: Having an insatiable appetite for food or activity; as, a *voracious* collector of baseball statistics. Latin *vorare* (to devour).

rapacious — D: Greedy; predatory; taking by force whatever one wants; as, a *rapacious* dictator. Latin *rapere* (to seize).

judicious — B: Wise; sensible; practical; as, *judicious* advice. Latin *judicium* (judgment).

judicial — B: Unbiased; fair; as, a *judicial* decision. Primarily of judges or a law court; as, the *judicial* system. Latin *judex* (judge).

cynical — C: Contemptuously distrustful; not believing in human goodness or sincerity. From the Cynics, ancient Greek philosophers thought of as self-righteous, misanthropic, even currish. Greek *kynos* (dog).

skeptical — D: Unconvinced; doubting; as, to be *skeptical* about a new medical cure. Greek *skeptikos* (reflective).

obtuse — D: Dull; insensitive; mentally slow; as, to be so *obtuse* as to ignore strong hints. Also, an angle greater than 90 degrees and less than 180. Latin *obtusus* (blunted).

abstruse — A: Difficult to understand; beyond average intelligence; as, an *abstruse* scientific concept. Latin *abstrudere* (to thrust away).

queue — B: Line of people waiting their turn. Also, a pigtail, or computer data "waiting in line" to be processed. Latin *cauda* (tail).

cue — C: Guiding suggestion; signal. Originally "Q" from Latin *quando* (when), written on scripts to indicate a character's entrance or action.

Vocabulary Ratings

9 — 11 correct . . . Good

12 — 17 correct . . . Excellent

18 — 20 correct . . . Exceptional

SPELLBOUND

I have a spelling checker,
It came with my PC;
It plainly marks four my revue
Mistakes I cannot sea.
I've run this poem threw it,
I'm sure your please too no,
Its letter perfect in it's weigh,
My checker tolled me sew.

—*QUOTED BY PENNYE HARPER*

This quiz contains a selection of "concept words"—expressions or phrases based on ideas and images. Concept words give us broader understandings and change the way we think and act. Try to catch the idea or image behind the following words. Turn the page to check your score.

anarchy *n.* — A: lawlessness. B: self-rule. C: mandate. D: ignorance.

networking *n.* — A: intense activism. B: development of contacts. C: illegal operation. D: projecting into outer space.

biodegradable *adj.* — A: endangered. B: capable of decomposing. C: offensively odorous. D: polluting.

symbiosis *n.* — A: similarity. B: cure-all. C: close association. D: transformation.

ecumenical *adj.* — A: helpful. B: relevant. C: universal. D: thrifty.

clone *v.* — A: to joke. B: exclude. C: revitalize. D: duplicate.

feminism *n.* — doctrine pertaining to women's A: obligations. B: rights. C: femininity. D: inherent strength.

supply-side economics — theory that emphasizes A: tax cuts. B: welfare. C: imports. D: exports.

black hole — A: moonless night. B: collapsed star. C: economic crisis. D: oceanic depression.

bluestocking *n.* — A: strongly religious woman. B: type of country music. C: high fashion. D: intellectual woman.

TAKE YOUR PIQUE
Courage: fear extinguisher —Ellis Stewart

Pessimist: one who no's too much—Franklin Krook

Smile: mirth mark —Daniel M. Evans

Boasting: patter of little feats—Marguerite Whitley May in *The Wall Street Journal*

Grouch potato: TV addict who grumbles when disturbed

—Shelby Friedman in *Quote* magazine

Heir styling: genetic engineering —Al Bernstein

Befaxed: beseiged by unsolicited fax messages

—Victor Navasky, quoted by William Grimes in *New York Times*

---

populist *n.* — promoter of A: conformity. B: mainstream politics. C: celebrities. D: the interests of ordinary people.

geopolitical *adj.* — concerning A: local politics. B: the military. C: politics and geography. D: nationalism.

relativity *n.* — theory concerning A: ethical judgments. B: family trees. C: balance. D: matter, energy, time and space.

dystopia (dis TOE pea ah) *n.* — A: wretched situation. B: place of magical charm. C: superstitious belief. D: type of illness.

karma *n.* — A: unexplained event. B: illusion. C: love. D: fate.

byzantine *adj.* — A: complex. B: peaceful. C: visionary. D: seductive.

ergonomics *n.* — study of A: population. B: economic growth. C: workplace design. D: industrial profits.

jihad *n.* — A: tribal custom. B: religious sect. C: jewel. D: Islamic holy war.

philistine *n.* — A: uncultured person. B: foreigner. C: one who is ingenious. D: selfish individual.

ecology *n.* — A: disease control. B: evolution. C: balance of nature. D: heredity.

IN OTHER WORDS

Goblet: young turkey —Jerri L. Nunn

Physiology: science of carbonating soft drinks —Nathan Fabling

Counter-attack: January sales —G. Pearson

Scotchguard: person watching the liquor cabinet —Charlie Reinke

 ANSWERS

anarchy — A: Lawlessness; absence of government control resulting in political disorder and sometimes violence. Greek *anarchos* (without a leader).

networking — B: The development and maintenance of personal contacts for exchanging information on topics of mutual interest, such as careers.

biodegradable — B: Capable of decomposing into harmless products; as, a new generation of *biodegradable* plastics. Greek *bios* (life) and Late Latin *degradare* (to reduce the rank of).

symbiosis — C: Close association of two unlike organisms resulting in advantage to both; as, A *symbiosis* exists between the rhinoceros and the birds that eat annoying ticks on its back. Greek (a living together).

ecumenical — C: Universal; worldwide; specifically, relating to religious unity. Also, interdenominational; as, The *ecumenical* meeting represented all major religious faiths. Greek *oikoumenikos* (of the whole world).

clone — D: To duplicate; to reproduce or propagate asexually. Also, to copy a computer design under another brand name. Greek *klon* (a twig).

feminism — B: Doctrine based on the view that women should be given the rights, opportunities and treatment accorded to men. Latin *femina* (woman).

supply-side economics — A: Theory holding that the economy will be stimulated by investment incentives, such as tax cuts.

black hole — B: Perhaps the invisible remains of a collapsed star with a gravitational field so intense that neither matter nor light can escape.

bluestocking — D: A woman with strong intellectual ability and literary interests. From the *blue stockings* worn by a member of an 18th-century London literary society.

populist — D: Promoter of the interests of ordinary people, as opposed to the elite. Many politicians claim to be *populists*. Latin *populus* (people).

geopolitical — C: Concerning the interrelationship of politics and geography, especially as it affects a nation's foreign policies. From German *Geopolitik*.

relativity — D: Theory developed by Albert Einstein explaining, among other things, relationships among matter, energy, time and space.

dystopia — A: A hypothetical situation or place where everything is wretched and the people are miserable. The opposite of utopia; as, The tiny nation had become a *dystopia*. Greek *dys-* (bad) and *topos* (place).

karma — D: Fate. For Hindus and Buddhists, one's actions bring inevitable results, good or bad, either in this life or in a reincarnation. Sanskrit (deed, act).

byzantine — A: Complex, devious and scheming; resembling the policies of the ancient Byzantine Empire.

ergonomics — C: Study of workplace and equipment designed to eliminate discomfort and fatigue. Greek *ergon* (work) and *-nomy* (arrangement, management).

jihad — D: Islamic holy war against unbelievers or enemies, undertaken as a religious duty. Arabic.

philistine — A: Uncultured, materialistic person with little interest in the arts. From Philistine, warlike inhabitant of ancient coastal Palestine.

ecology — C: Balance of nature; study of the interrelationship of organisms and their environment. Greek *oikos* (habitat) and *-logy* (study of).

Vocabulary Ratings

9 — 11 correct . . . Good

12 — 17 correct . . . Excellent

18 — 20 correct . . . Exceptional

PROFITS WITH INTEREST

Words are assets you can bank on. Use the following list to see if you make a verbal profit. Turn the page to get to the bottom line.

naïve *adj.* — A: refreshingly direct. B: reserved and cool.
C: unsophisticated. D: carefree.

dilemma *n.* — A: catastrophe. B: reluctance to act. C: perplexing
situation. D: desperation.

serape (suh RAH pee) *n.* — A: blanket used as a poncho.
B: sharp reply. C: brief rest. D: carrying case.

retrograde *adj.* — A: backward. B: smooth. C: level. D: advanced.

fiat (FEE at) *n.* — A: technological feat. B: arbitrary decree.
C: power. D: culmination.

montage (mahn TAZH) *n.* — A: large screen. B: actor's monologue.
C: elongated balcony. D: composite picture.

adept *adj.* — A: confident. B: quick. C: skillful. D: effortless.

immemorial *adj.* — A: complimentary. B: ancient. C: unremarkable.
D: not to be forgotten.

mollify *v.* — A: to pacify. B: disguise. C: gladden. D: enhance.

recount *v.* — A: to be long-winded. B: synthesize. C: ignore.
D: tell in detail.

QUIP WITS

One day I called my broker about a stock that had been down
in the dumps. "Do you think I'll live to see it go higher?" I
asked. "Frankly," he said, "I wish you were a younger man."

—*Contributed by Donald S. Reiss*

> **❝**We are all born into the world with nothing. Everything we acquire after that is profit.**❞**
>
> —SAM EWING

---

coin *v.* — A: to evaluate anew. B: imitate. C: invent. D: abscond.

indiscreet *adj.* — A: unwise. B: confused. C: humorously inconsistent. D: frenzied.

attest *v.* — A: to challenge. B: depend on. C: confirm. D: qualify.

variance *n.* — A: congruence. B: comparison. C: flexibility. D: difference.

minatory (MIN uh tor ee) *adj.* — A: pertaining to fish. B: threatening. C: insignificant. D: haughty.

frugal *adj.* — A: quiet. B: obstinate. C: efficient. D: thrifty.

precept *n.* — A: feeling or prediction. B: legal decision. C: rule of conduct. D: idea.

surcease *n.* — A: lengthy explanation. B: cessation. C: something added. D: extreme situation.

homily *n.* — A: sermon. B: pithy saying. C: peaceful atmosphere. D: epic poem.

preternatural (pree tur NACH ur'l) *adj.* — A: primitive. B: supernatural. C: spontaneous. D: artificial.

MAKING ALLOWANCES

To make the kids do what we want

We must be real inventive;

In Grandma's day 'twas called a bribe

Today it's an incentive.

—JUDI O'SULLIVAN

ANSWERS

naïve — C: Unsophisticated; simple; innocent. French, from *naïf* (natural).

dilemma — C: Perplexing, unavoidable situation in which a choice must be made between two equally undesirable alternatives. Greek *di-* (two) and *lemma* (proposition).

serape — A: Woolen blanket used as an outer garment in Latin America, especially Mexico. From Mexican-Spanish.

retrograde — A: Backward; as, The planet exhibited *retrograde* motion through the constellations. Latin *retro-* (backward) and *gradi* (to walk).

fiat — B: Arbitrary decree; authoritative order; as, The tyrant's *fiat* sent troops into a neighboring country. Latin (let it be done).

montage — D: Composite picture made by superimposing one element on another; as, a *montage* of notables. French, from *monter* (to mount).

adept — C: Skillful; proficient; as, The older couples were *adept* dancers. Latin *adipisci* (to attain).

immemorial — B: Ancient; beyond memory or record; as, The sexes have been battling since time *immemorial*. Latin *in-* (without) and *memoria* (memory).

mollify — A: To pacify; soothe; as, to *mollify* an angry customer. Latin *mollis* (soft).

recount — D: To tell in detail; give a full account of; as, Our daughter and her husband *recounted* their diving experience near a killer whale. French *re-* (again) and *conter* (to relate).

coin — C: To invent a word or phrase; as, Our friend *coined* "flustrated" to express flustered frustration. Old French *coign* (metal stamp).

indiscreet — A: Unwise; lacking good judgment; thoughtless; as, Blurting out a secret is *indiscreet*. Latin *indiscretus* (unseparated).

attest — C: To confirm; declare to be genuine; as, The students' test scores *attest* to their teacher's skill. Latin *attestari* (to bear witness).

variance — D: Difference; deviation; as, a *variance* between two accounts of the game. Also, permission to bypass certain regulations. Latin *variare* (to vary, alter).

minatory — B: Threatening; menacing; as, a *minatory* forecast of violent thunderstorms. Latin *minari* (to threaten).

frugal — D: Thrifty; not wasteful; as, My *frugal* grandmother kept odds and ends of threads for a rainy day. Latin *frux* (profit).

precept — C: Rule or guiding principle of conduct; as, The *precept* "waste not, want not" takes on new meaning. Latin *prae-* (before) and *capere* (to take).

surcease — B: Cessation; as, Sometimes we need *surcease* from the many issues vying for our attention. French *surseoir* (to suspend).

homily — A: Sermon or discourse on a moral or religious topic. Greek *homilos* (assembly).

preternatural — B: Supernatural; beyond what is normal; as, With *preternatural* strength she freed her husband, who was pinned under the car. Latin *praeternaturalis*.

Vocabulary Ratings
9 — 11 correct . . . Good
12 — 17 correct . . . Excellent
18 — 20 correct . . . Exceptional

66There are no shortcuts to any place worth going.**99**

—*BEVERLY SILLS*

BIG BANGS

Don't miss the chance to put a big bang in your conversation with strong, effective words like those listed below. How many of them do you know? Turn the page to find your score.

acumen (a KYOO men) *n.* — A: exactness. B: potential.
    C: shrewdness. D: assurance.

premonition *n.* — A: understanding. B: forewarning.
    C: determination. D: mistrust.

criterion *n.* — A: explanation. B: essence. C: standard.
    D: turning point.

parlous *adj.* — A: exceedingly polite. B: timid. C: talkative.
    D: dangerous.

extricate *v.* — A: to frustrate. B: isolate. C: get rid of. D: set free.

myriad (MIR ee ud) *adj.* — A: assorted. B: colorful.
    C: vast in number. D: demanding.

analogue (AN uh log) *n.* — A: detailed analysis. B: something similar. C: chronological record. D: something opposite.

picayune (pik uh YOON) *adj.* — A: trivial. B: peculiar.
    C: adventurous. D: fussy.

adage *n.* — A: advantage. B: wise elder. C: enlargement.
    D: proverb.

behest *n.* — A: something handed down. B: equality. C: good turn.
    D: urgent request.

66The kind of humor I like is the thing that makes me laugh for five seconds and think for ten minutes.**99**

—WILLIAM DAVIS

❝Talent is a flame. Genius is a fire.❞

—BERN WILLIAMS

---

cobble *v.* — A: to hinder. B: strike out. C: make hastily. D: withdraw.

vintage *adj.* — A: outdated. B: classic or characteristic. C: traditionally suitable. D: ingenious.

segment *n.* — A: arc. B: solid residue. C: classification. D: section.

torpid *adj.* — A: hot and heavy. B: rapid. C: sluggish. D: dangerous.

penultimate (pih NUL tih mit) *adj.* — A: next to last. B: opposing. C: extreme. D: finest.

viability *n.* — A: availability. B: effectiveness. C: rationality. D: qualification.

emblematic *adj.* — A: symbolic. B: decorated. C: carefully outlined. D: significant.

roil *v.* — A: to clarify. B: wrap around. C: make muddy. D: detonate.

infallible *adj.* — A: obnoxiously confident. B: very stubborn. C: unbelievable. D: absolutely trustworthy.

crescendo (krih SHEN doh) *n.* — A: wavy motion. B: gradual increase. C: shrillness. D: decreasing pace.

DEFINE POINTS

Rare book: One that comes back after you've lent it.

—A. BRAITHWAITE

Split second: That brief moment in time between reading the freeway sign and realizing you've missed the off ramp.

—SAM EWING

 ANSWERS

acumen — C: Shrewdness; keenness and insight in understanding and handling practical affairs; as, having financial *acumen*. Latin *acuere* (to sharpen).

premonition — B: Forewarning; hunch something bad may happen; as, The mother's *premonition* of danger saved her daughter. Latin *praemonere* (to warn beforehand).

criterion — C: Standard or rule for evaluating something; as, a *criterion* for employment. Greek *kriterion* (means of judging).

parlous — D: Dangerous; risky; perilous; as, The ravaged nation is in *parlous* condition. Middle English contraction of *perilous*.

extricate — D: To set free from a difficulty; disentangle; as, to *extricate* oneself from an embarrassing situation. Latin *extricare*.

myriad — C: Vast in number; innumerable; as, *myriad* requests for assistance. Greek *myriados* (ten thousand).

analogue — B: Something similar; as, There is no *analogue* for the rapid world changes we are witnessing today. Greek *analogos* (in proportion).

picayune — A: Trivial; trifling; of small importance; as, He doesn't fuss over *picayune* details. Louisiana French *picaillon* (small coin).

adage — D: Proverb; traditional, popular saying expressing a general truth; as, the old *adage* "Live and let live." Latin *adagium*, related to *aio* (I say).

behest — D: Urgent request; command; as, at the *behest* of the President. Old English *behaes* (vow).

cobble — C: To make or compose in a hasty or clumsy way; as, The small country *cobbled* together a temporary survival program. From *cobbler*.

vintage — B: Classic; characteristic of a particular era; as, The dress code was *vintage* 1960s. Also, produced in a particular wine year. Latin *vinum* (wine).

segment — D: One of the sections or parts into which something can be separated; as, *segments* of an insect's body. Latin *secare* (to cut).

torpid — C: Sluggish; slow; apathetic; dull; as, the committee's *torpid* indifference to the request. Latin *torpere* (to be numb, inert).

penultimate — A: Next to last; as, The *penultimate* scene was the most moving in the play. Latin *paene* (almost) and *ultimus* (last).

viability — B: Effectiveness; ability to succeed or survive; as, The senator wanted to retain her political *viability*. Latin *vita* (life).

emblematic — A: Symbolic; serving as an emblem; as, The monetary conference is *emblematic* of international cooperation. Greek *emblema* (raised ornament).

roil — C: To make muddy by stirring up sediment; hence, also, to irritate, make angry; as, She did not allow herself to be *roiled* by his remarks. Old French *rouil* (rust, mud).

infallible — D: Absolutely trustworthy; never failing; unerring; as, an *infallible* remedy, guide or memory. Latin *infallibilis*.

crescendo — B: Gradual increase in loudness or intensity; as, the *crescendo* of fierce winds. Latin *crescere* (to arise, grow).

Vocabulary Ratings
>   9 — 11 correct ... Good
>   12 — 17 correct ... Excellent
>   18 — 20 correct ... Exceptional

FIREWORKS
Fabulous yellow
Roman candles exploding
Like spiders across the stars
And in the middle you see
The blue centerlight pop
And everybody goes "Awww!"

—JACK KEROUAC

ON SECOND THOUGHT

The English language has some confusing rules of pronunciation. Consider such look-alike words as though, bough, *and* enough, *and the fact that sometimes there are several meanings for words that sound the same. How do you pronounce the following, sometimes tricky words? And do you know their meanings? Turn the page to find your score.*

gnarled *adj.* — A: carelessly thrown together. B: having knobby lumps. C: smooth. D: hacked up.

fjord *n.* — A: snow-covered mountain. B: narrow inlet between cliffs. C: musical instrument. D: Norwegian folk tale.

timbre *n.* — A: characteristic tone. B: particular rhythm. C: construction material. D: tensile strength.

rancor *n.* — A: despair. B: disillusionment. C: jubilation. D: resentment.

aegis *n.* — A: protection. B: dramatic poem. C: channel. D: framework.

berserk *adj.* — A: awkward. B: odd. C: frenzied. D: careless.

comparable *adj.* — A: greater. B: clear. C: less. D: similar.

dais *n.* — A: receptacle for flowers. B: platform for speakers. C: reading desk. D: front of a building.

germane *adj.* — A: graceful. B: relevant. C: harmonious. D: illusory.

kudos *n.* — A: Oriental martial art. B: African animal. C: praise. D: massage.

unctuous *adj.* — A: contented to a fault. B: kindly and caring. C: pretending   sincerity. D: perfumed.

66When my fifth grade class came indoors after playing, I noticed that one boy had a red mark around his neck. It had been caused, he explained, when his scarf was pulled off his neck. Quite impressed with the injury, he exclaimed, 'I was almost decaffeinated!'**99**

—Kim Herr

---

vignette *n.* — A: sauce or dressing. B: small eyeglasses. C: delicate vase. D: short description.

docile *adj.* — A: peaceful. B: amorous. C: ineffectual. D: submissive.

onus *n.* — A: singleness of purpose. B: prophetic sign. C: burden. D: obstacle.

patina *n.* — A: outside dining area. B: surface film. C: dialect. D: scatter rug.

vagary *n.* — A: contrariness. B: irritating slowness. C: whim. D: fuzzy thought.

critique *n.* — A: detailed summary. B: severe scolding. C: irrefutable proof.   D: thorough evaluation.

essay *v.* — A: to try. B: resign. C: divert. D: suggest.

prescient *adj.* — A: primitive. B: obtuse. C: having an inkling of future events. D: bright and cheerful.

pseudonym *n.* — A: fictitious name. B: dietary supplement. C: subtle lie. D: secret message.

WRONG MOTS
"Today we learned the Heimlich remover."

—Quoted by Lynith G. Brown

 *ANSWERS*

gnarled (NARLD) — **B:** Having knobby lumps; twisted, bent; as a *gnarled* tree trunk. Middle English *knor* (a swelling).

fjord (FYOHRD) — **B:** Long, narrow, deep inlet from the sea between cliffs, as in Norway. Old Icelandic *fjordhr*.

timbre (TAM bur) — **A:** Characteristic tone; distinctive quality of a voice or an instrument; as, the sweet *timbre* of her voice. Old French (a kind of drum).

rancor (RANG kor) — **D:** Bitter, long-lasting resentment or hatred; as the *rancor* Croatian and Serbian troops felt for each other. Latin *rancere* (to stink, be rancid).

aegis (EE jis) — **A:** Protection; as, relief supplies sent under the *aegis* of the United Nations. Also, sponsorship. Greek *aigis* (shield).

berserk (bur ZURK) — **C:** Frenzied and emotionally upset to a violent extent; as, Teased mercilessly, the dog went *berserk*. Old Icelandic *berserkr* (wild warrior in a bearskin).

comparable (KOM puh ruh b'l) — **D:** Similar; equivalent; as, The two nations have *comparable* regimes. Latin *com-* (together) and *par* (equal).

dais (DAY is) — **B:** Raised platform for speakers or guests of honor. Middle English *deis* (high table in a hall).

germane (jur MAYN) — **B:** Relevant; appropriate or fitting; as, arguments *germane* to the issue. Latin *germanus* (having the same parents).

kudos (KOO dohz, KYOO dohz) — **C:** Praise, honor or acclaim for achievement; as, The teacher deserved her *kudos*. Greek *kydos* (glory or fame).

unctuous (UNGK choo us) — **C:** Pretending sincerity with a smug or virtuous demeanor, often with an oily charm; as, an *unctuous* con artist. Latin *ungere* (to anoint).

vignette (vin YET) — **D:** Short, graceful description or memorable scene; as, character *vignettes* in a film. Also, decorative design or a picture with no definite edge. French *vigne* (vine).

docile (DOSS uhl) — **D:** Submissive; easy to manage or discipline; as, a *docile* pony. Latin *docere* (to teach).

onus (OH nus) — **C:** Difficult burden or responsibility that may cause anxiety or hardship; blame; as, the *onus* of making a life-and-death decision. Latin.

patina (puh TEE nuh, PAT'n uh) — **B:** Surface film produced by age or use; greenish incrustation on copper or bronze. Italian (tarnish).

vagary (VAY guh ree, vuh GAIR ee) — **C:** Whim; unpredictable, often irresponsible, act or idea; as, the *vagaries* of fate. Latin *vagari* (to wander).

critique (krih TEEK) — **D:** Thorough evaluation, particularly of a work of art or literature. Greek *kritikos* (able to discern).

essay (eh SAY) — **A:** To try, especially a difficult task; as, to *essay* a new beginning in a science-fiction story. Old French *essai* (trial).

prescient (PRESH ee unt, PREE she unt) — **C:** Having an inkling of future events; as, a *prescient* economist. Latin *praescire* (to know beforehand).

pseudonym (SUE duh nim, SEUD'n im) — **A:** Fictitious name taken by a writer; as, John Le Carré is the *pseudonym* of English author David John Moore Cornwell. Greek *pseudo* (false) and *onyma* (name).

Vocabulary Ratings

> **9 — 11 correct . . . Good**
> **12 — 17 correct . . . Excellent**
> **18 — 20 correct . . . .Exceptional**

FRACTURED PHRASES

"I think his wife would leave him at the slightest prevarication."

—John Scott Fones

HIDDEN MEANINGS

Digging out the definition of each word you're curious about is a good way to "bone up" on your vocabulary. Test yourself against this list of colorful, exotic and practical words. Then turn the page to find your results.

seascape *n.* — A: wave top. B: ocean debris. C: picture. D: boating accident.

aficionado (uh fish yuh NAH doh) *n.* — A: expert. B: good friend. C: guide. D: ardent fan.

facsimile (fac SIM uh lee) *n.* — A: fake. B: model or example. C: nostrum. D: exact copy.

implode *v.* — A: to load. B: burst inward. C: laminate. D: instigate to action.

impresario *n.* — A: magician. B: mountebank. C: manager. D: impersonator.

barrio *n.* — A: leather thong. B: Spanish-American food. C: Spanish-speaking neighborhood. D: horse-training corral.

indelible adj. — A: permanent. B: beyond doubt. C: impenetrable. D: eradicable.

inveigle (in VEE guhl, in VAY guhl) *v.* — A: to complicate. B: entice. C: break into. D: denounce.

marauding *adj.* — A: parading. B: wandering aimlessly. C: brawling. D: raiding.

database *n.* — A: starting point. B: system of signals. C: collection of information. D: domicile.

ROUNDABOUTS

Double occupancy means two can stay as cheaply as one who has to pay double if he's alone. —Ralph Shaffer

> **"**Nowadays, when you get right down to brass tacks, they're plastic.**"**
>
> —GIL STERN

ensemble (ahn SAHM b'l) *n.* — A: sacred music. B: old-fashioned dance. C: musical fanfare. D: group of performers.

commodious *adj.* — A: spacious. B: sheltering. C: well-supplied. D: comfortable.

stymie *v.* — A: to hinder. B: stimulate. C: confuse. D: disgrace.

flair *n.* — A: emergency signal. B: enthusiasm. C: lighthearted bravado. D: natural ability.

replete *adj.* — A: embellished. B: reworked. C: abounding. D: lacking energy.

genial *adj.* — A: spontaneous. B: kindly. C: fascinating. D: ingratiating.

communiqué (kuh MEW nuh kay) *n.* — A: propaganda. B: cipher. C: announcement. D: indiscretion.

slough (SLUFF) *v.* — A: to botch. B: ignore. C: slouch. D: shed.

retaliation *n.* — A: keeping score. B: repayment in kind. C: open disrespect. D: long-lasting hatred.

militant *adj.* — A: aggressive. B: opinionated. C: practical. D: organized.

FEAR ITSELF
Fobia: fear of misspelled words —Charles Burgess
Hype-ochondria: fear of TV commercials —Jacqueline Schiff
Tripidation: fear of traveling —Hank Billings
Auldlanxiety: fear of New Year's Eve —Bonnie Pastoor

ANSWERS

seascape — C: Picture, sketch, painting or photograph of the sea; as, The artist Winslow Homer was noted for his *seascapes*. Variation of *landscape*.

aficionado — D: Ardent fan, supporter or devotee; as, a crossword-puzzle *aficionado*. Spanish *aficionar* (to arouse affection).

facsimile — D: Exact copy or reproduction. Also, method of transmitting graphic matter electronically by telephone line. Latin *fac simile* (to make similar).

implode — B: To burst or collapse violently inward; as, The robot submarine *imploded* and sank. Latin *in-* (in, within) and *plaudere* (to clap, beat or stamp).

impresario — C: Manager, producer or organizer of public entertainment, especially concerts, opera or ballet. Italian *imprendere* (to undertake).

barrio — C: Spanish-speaking neighborhood. In Hispanic countries, a district or suburb of a city. Arabic *barr* (open area).

indelible — A: Permanent; incapable of being erased or removed; as, *indelible* ink. Also, unforgettable; as, *indelible* memories. Latin *indelebilis* (indestructible).

inveigle — B: To entice or persuade by trickery or cleverness; tempt; as, to *inveigle* someone into a bad investment. Middle French *aveugler* (to delude, make blind).

marauding — D: Raiding and ravaging an area in search of plunder and the like; as, *marauding* troops. French *maraud* (rascal, tomcat).

database — C: Comprehensive collection of electronic information designed for quick computerized retrieval and updating; as, a *database* of potential customers' names.

ensemble — D: Group of entertainers who perform together; as, a brass *ensemble*. Also, term for a well-matched outfit of clothes. Late Latin *insimul* (at the same time).

commodious — A: Spacious and roomy; as, to hold the meeting in the *commodious* old ballroom. Latin *commodus* (convenient).

stymie — A: To hinder or thwart; as, The recession *stymied* economic growth. Scottish origin.

flair — D: Natural ability, talent or knack; as, the columnist's *flair* for the apt word. Also, stylishness; as, to dress with *flair*. Old French *flairer* (to give off an odor or scent).

replete — C: Abounding; plentifully supplied; as, a resort *replete* with night life, sports and good food. Also, gorged or sated. Latin *replere* (to fill up).

genial — B: Kindly, pleasant and cheerful; as, *genial* grandparents. Latin *genius* (guardian, deity).

communiqué — C: Announcement; official communication or bulletin reporting an event; as, A *communiqué* was issued after the summit meeting. From French *communiquer* (to inform).

slough — D: Shed; get rid or dispose of; cast off; as, At ease now, she *sloughed* off her fears. German *Schlauch* (a skin).

retaliation — B: Repayment in kind, especially for a wrong or an injury; a getting even; as, Martin Luther King, Jr., encouraged love, not *retaliation*. Latin *retaliare*.

militant — A: Aggressive and vigorous in support of a cause; as, a *militant* political activist. Also, warlike. Latin *militare* (to serve as a soldier).

Vocabulary Ratings
> 9 — 11 correct . . . Good
> 12 — 17 correct . . . Excellent
> 18 — 20 correct . . . Exceptional

66Vision is the art of seeing things invisible.**99**

—Jonathan Swift

Here's a collection of words taken from several crossword puzzles and brain teasers. Match wits with the puzzle constructors and select the answer you think is correct. Turn the page for your score.

pomp *n.* — A: self-assurance. B: fame. C: stately display. D: upswept hair style.

guru *n.* — A: African antelope. B: spiritual adviser. C: gifted person. D: deceptive gambler.

retrench *v.* — A: to establish. B: economize. C: dig out. D: fill in with earth.

précis (PRAY see) *n.* — A: summary. B: correct method. C: advance showing. D: prediction.

modish *adj.* — A: fashionable. B: temperamental. C: snobbish. D: shy.

ilk *n.* — A: source. B: sickness. C: small group. D: same kind.

medley *n.* — A: recurring theme. B: assortment of items. C: average result. D: softness.

allay *v.* — A: to join. B: state to be true. C: calm. D: retreat from.

prevail *v.* — A: to beg. B: prevent. C: grasp. D: triumph.

dam *n.* — A: woman of nobility. B: great strength. C: animal's female parent. D: counteraction.

askance *adv.* — with A: horror. B: suspicion. C: awkwardness. D: coyness.

66The world's major trouble spots these days were formerly known only to crossword-puzzle fans.**99**

—VAL TUPY, QUOTED BY JACK ROSENBAUM IN SAN FRANCISCO INDEPENDENT

WIT BITS

Kids' bedtime: pajama drama —Connie Theis

Fast-food restaurant: economy gastronomy —David E. Reilly

Proofreader: blooper snooper —Doreen Clendenen

---

tinge *v.* — A: to burn. B: make a light, ringing sound.
  C: color slightly. D: spoil or corrupt.

wan *adj.* — A: pale. B: tender. C: unexpressive. D: thin.

bauble *n.* — A: foolish talk. B: small bubble. C: social error.
  D: worthless trinket.

par *n.* — A: superior attainment. B: figure of speech. C: smallness.
  D: average condition.

prig *n.* — person who is A: boring. B: self-righteous. C: gossipy.
  D: witty.

riff *n.* — A: animation. B: rupture of a relationship.
  C: disreputable person. D: repeated melodic phrase.

downy *adj.* — A: soft and fluffy. B: foolish and flighty.
  C: somewhat seedy. D: languid or flabby.

mote *n.* — A: wide ditch. B: emotional outburst. C: speck.
  D: act of shedding.

lulu *n.* — A: Polynesian feast. B: euphemism for washroom. C:
  lucky break. D: anything remarkable.

CAUGHT IN THE RIDDLE

Q: What do you get when you cross the language barrier?

A: A phonic boom.

—MORRIS G. HULTS

ANSWERS

pomp — C: Stately display. Also, ostentatious showiness. Greek *pompe* (solemn procession).

guru — B: Spiritual adviser, teacher or highly regarded leader (sometimes used derisively); as, a literary *guru*. Sanskrit (weighty, venerable).

retrench — B: To economize; reduce or curtail expenses. Old French *re-* (back) and *trenchier* (to cut).

précis — A: Concise summary of the essentials; as, a *précis* of one's employment background. Latin *praecidere* (to shorten).

modish — A: Fashionable; in the latest style; trendy; as, *modish* jewelry. French *mode* (fashion, vogue) and English *-ish* (pertaining to).

ilk — D: The same kind, sort, class. Often used in a belittling sense; as, Imagine inviting people of that *ilk*! Old English *ilca* (same).

medley — B: Assortment of unrelated items; hodgepodge. Old French *medlee*.

allay — C: To calm or quiet fears and the like; as, to *allay* the dread of being abandoned. Old English *alecgan* (to put down).

prevail — D: To triumph; dominate; as, She *prevailed* against all odds. Also, to be widespread; as, Happiness *prevailed*. Or, to use persuasion successfully; as, He *prevailed* upon us to go. Latin *praevalere* (to be stronger).

dam — C: Female parent of any four-legged animal, especially domestic animals; as, the famous *dam* of a champion Thoroughbred horse. Thirteenth-century variation of *dame*.

askance — B: With suspicion, mistrust, disapproval; as, She looked *askance* at the huckster. Also, a sideways glance. Middle English *ascaunce* (as if).

tinge — C: To color slightly; as, a sunset *tinged* with pink. Also, to add a trace; as, joy *tinged* with regret. Latin *tingere*.

wan — A: Pale, from illness, exhaustion or deep unhappiness; as, her *wan*, haggard face. Old English *wann* (dark, gloomy).

bauble — D: Worthless, showy trinket; any useless thing; as, *baubles* wrapped in expensive-looking boxes. Old French *baubel* (toy).

par — D: Average or normal condition; as, feeling up to *par*. Also, face value of bonds, etc.; standard for golf strokes; an equal footing; as, on a *par* with one's peers. Latin (equal).

prig — B: Person who is self-righteous or smug about assumed superior virtues and wisdom. British slang; origin unknown.

riff — D: In jazz, a repeated melodic phrase as a background accompaniment for a soloist. Probably from *refrain*.

downy — A: Soft and fluffy; as, a downy pillow. From English *down* (young duck's feathers).

mote — C: Speck or particle; as, "And why beholdest thou the *mote* that is in thy brother's eye, but considerest not the beam that is in thine own eye?" Old English *mot*.

lulu — D: Anyone or anything remarkable or outstanding, as a beautiful girl, windstorm, examination and the like. U.S. slang, probably from the nickname for *Louise*.

Vocabulary Ratings
> 9 — 11 correct . . . Good
> 12 — 17 correct . . . Excellent
> 18 — 20 correct . . . Exceptional

COLLECTIVELY SPEAKING

A raft of survivors —Larry Mills

A drove of cars —Ruth Ann Esch

A pound of hammers —Louis Phillips

WORDPLAY

Wordplay can be endlessly fascinating. For example, in this quiz of paired words, when you substitute just one letter for another, you end up with an entirely new word. Choose the meaning you think is correct for each. Turn the page for your score.

sear *v.* — A: to insult. B: thirst. C: predict. D: scorch.

seer *n.* — A: elderly person. B: cooking utensil. C: idealist.
D: prophet.

dun *v.* — A: to soil. B: add to. C: demand payment. D: find fault.

don *v.* — A: to chaperone. B: put on. C: give. D: lord over.

nib *n.* — A: point. B: small amount. C: essence. D: clever response.

nub *n.* — A: clumsy person. B: lack of courtesy.
C: mechanical fitting. D: knob or lump.

vie (VY) *v.* — A: to long for. B: compete. C: urge. D: pass through.

via *prep.* — A: over. B: toward. C: by way of. D: between.

quark *n.* — A: in physics, a fundamental particle. B: unusual star.
C: newt. D: any unexplained phenomenon.

quirk *n.* — A: dagger. B: self-satisfied smile. C: odd mannerism.
D: habit.

couch *v.* — A: to camouflage. B: put into words. C: relax.
D: hunker down.

NINETIES NOMENCLATURE

Shamnesia: fake memory lapse —Ellis Stewart

Slugvest: bulletproof jacket —B. J. Thompson

Ecomaniac: environmental activist —Wesley G. Hunt

WORRY WORDS

Hamnesia: bad actor's memory lapse —Shelby Friedman

Angoraphobia: fear of furry sweaters —Brian Todd Simmons

Fee-fie-fo-bia: fear of giants —Virginia Ebright

---

conch (KONK; KONCH) *n.* — A: part of a saddle. B: crown. C: rope. D: shell.

wax *v.* — A: to begin. B: diminish. C: melt. D: grow.

wag *n.* — A: sprite. B: dishonest person. C: joker. D: someone who is ineffectual.

score *v.* — A: to criticize severely. B: cleanse. C: flatter. D: treat with deference.

scope *n.* — A: agenda. B: range or extent. C: educated guess. D: conclusion.

rife *adj.* — A: divided. B: petty. C: widespread. D: accurate.

rile *v.* — A: to enliven. B: waste time. C: blunder. D: annoy.

chafe *v.* — A: to rub against. B: tease. C: cut through. D: challenge persistently.

chaff *n.* — A: compost. B: impatience. C: grain husks. D: foolishness.

WHAT DO YOU CALL . . .

. . . the guy who understands everything you say? Roger

—Joseph P. Lassegard

. . . the fellow you find lying on your porch? Matt

—Janet Blamford

. . . the woman who never stands up straight? Eileen

—John Lynch

 *ANSWERS*

sear — D: To scorch; brown quickly; wither; as, The summer sun can *sear* a field. Old English *searian* (to dry).

seer — D: Prophet; one who predicts; wise person; someone with deep moral and spiritual insight. Middle English *seen* (to see).

dun — C: To demand payment of a debt; as, Credit-card companies *dun* delinquent customers. Perhaps derived from Joe Dun, a 16th-century London debt collector.

don — B: To put on; as, They quickly *donned* raincoats and left. Contraction of *do* and *on*.

nib — A: Point of anything; as, the *nib* of a pen; the diamond *nib* of a record player. Old English *nebb* (beak).

nub — D: Knob or lump. Also, the gist, heart or point of something; as, the *nub* of a discussion. Middle Low German *knubbe* (knot).

vie — B: To compete; struggle for superiority; as, tennis rivals *vying* for a championship. Old French *envier* (to challenge).

via — C: By way of; through; as, to go from New York to San Francisco *via* Chicago. Also, by means of; as, *via* airmail. Latin.

quark — A: In physics, a fundamental particle of which protons and neutrons are made. Coined from a line in James Joyce's *Finnegans Wake*: "Three *quarks* for Muster Mark."

quirk — C: Odd mannerism or trait; idiosyncrasy; as, her *quirk* of talking to house plants. Also, sudden change or twist; as, to win by a *quirk* of fate. Origin unknown.

couch — B: To put into words; express; as, She *couched* her request in an amusing way. Old French *coucher* (to lay down).

conch — D: Large, handsome, spiral shell of various marine mollusks. Greek *konche*.

wax — D: To grow, as said of the moon. Also, to increase in intensity; as, to *wax* enthusiastic over an idea. Old English *weaxan*.

wag — C: Joker; wisecracker; wit. Perhaps shortened from Middle English *waghalter* (rogue, rascal or mischievous person; also, someone likely to hang).

score — A: To criticize severely; berate; as, The media *scored* the senator's poor judgment. Old Norse *skora* (to notch).

scope — B: Range or extent; as, within the *scope* of his ability. Also, opportunity; as, the exciting *scope* of the plan. Greek *scopos* (aim, target).

rife — C: Widespread, suggesting an increase of something; as, a city *rife* with drug-related crime. Old English *ryfe* (abundant).

rile — D: To annoy; vex; irk; as, People were *riled* over the unexpected increase in taxes. Variation of *roil* (to stir up).

chafe — A: To rub against, making sore or worn; as, The stiff collar *chafed* her neck. Also, to become impatient; as, He *chafed* at restrictions. Middle English *chaufen* (to warm).

chaff — C: Grain husks separated from seeds by threshing. Also, banter or good-natured teasing. Middle English *chaf*.

Vocabulary Ratings

    9 — 11 correct . . . Good
    12 — 17 correct . . . Excellent
    18 — 20 correct . . . Exceptional

WOULD YOU SAY THAT . . .

. . . people who sell perfume are always sticking their business in your nose? —Ink Inc.

. . . the U.S. trade deficit is news of considerable import?
—Bill Tammeus in Kansas City Star

Few mystery writers use vocabulary with greater skill than P. D. James. The following words are taken from her book  Devices and Desires. *How good a word sleuth are you in tracking down the correct meanings? Turn the page to find your score.*

pallid *adj.* — A: gloomy or sad. B: smooth and glowing.
C: lacking color. D: submissive.

cumbersome *adj.* — A: obnoxious. B: sluggish. C: unwieldy.
D: diminutive.

raucous *adj.* — A: piercing. B: undercooked. C: loud and harsh.
D: vulgar.

cursory *adj.* — A: obscene. B: crafty. C: mean. D: superficial.

clutch *n.* — A: cluster. B: keyhole. C: obvious clue. D: small cage.

concomitant *adj.* — A: resulting. B: occurring together.
C: fully committed. D: understandable.

reticent *adj.* — A: pure. B: furtive. C: reserved. D: effusive.

condolences *n.* — A: congratulations. B: expressions of sympathy.
C: words of forgiveness. D: acts of conciliation.

ostensibly *adv.* — A: virtually. B: obviously. C: strictly.
D: apparently.

sobriquet (SO bruh kay) *n.* — A: actress in a light comedy.
B: witty remark. C: type of painting. D: nickname.

WORDS TO THE WISE

Murder mysteries in print, like crossword puzzles and chocolate, are little getaways of certainty and comfort.

—JOHN DOUGLAS, *QUOTED BY* AMY CLYDE *IN* NEW YORK TIMES

CAUGHT IN THE RIDDLE

Q: Why is a good writer like a criminal?

A: Because they both prefer short sentences.

—RICHARD CRASTA

---

lugubrious (luh GOO bree us) *adj.* — A: mournful. B: greasy.
C: fawning. D: slow and heavy.

frisson *n.* — A: shudder. B: calm. C: decorative border.
D: type of dessert.

venue (VEN yoo) *n.* — A: recollection. B: meeting place.
C: passageway. D: long vista.

recrimination *n.* — A: setback. B: rebirth. C: countercharge.
D: asperity.

vicarious (vy KAIR ee us) *adj.* — A: many and varied. B: doubtful.
C: transitory. D: serving as a substitute.

histrionic *adj.* — A: hypersensitive. B: historically significant.
C: uncouth. D: excessively dramatic.

derisory (dih RY suh ree) *adj.* — A: amusing. B: unfortunate.
C: ridiculous. D: damaging.

unprepossessing *adj.* — A: poverty-stricken. B: unimpressive.
C: distinctive. D: laid-back.

condone *v.* — A: to forgive. B: eliminate. C: regret. D: advise.

rail *v.* — A: to rush through. B: punish. C: attack verbally.
D: lament.

66The difference between the impossible and the
possible lies in a person's determination.**99**

—TOMMY LASORDA

 *ANSWERS*

pallid — C: Lacking color, vitality or interest; as, "He recalled Blaney's *pallid* and innocuous watercolors." Latin *pallidus*.

cumbersome — C: Unwieldy; as, "her *cumbersome* shoulder bag flapping against her ribs." Old French *combrer* (to hinder).

raucous — C: Loud and harsh; rowdy; as, "the *raucous* beat of the music." Latin *raucus* (hoarse).

cursory — D: Superficial; hasty; as, "a *cursory* glance at the serial killer." Latin *currere* (to run).

clutch — A: A cluster, group or bunch; as, "a *clutch* of chief constables." Old Norse *klekja* (to hatch).

concomitant — B: Occurring together; accompanying; as, "Success has its *concomitant* disadvantages." Latin *concomitari* (to follow).

reticent — C: Reserved; not speaking openly or revealing one's thoughts. Latin *reticere* (to be silent).

condolences — B: Expressions of sympathy or comfort; as, "a formal visit of *condolence*." Latin *com-* (with) and *dolere* (to grieve).

ostensibly — D: Apparently but not necessarily so; as, *Ostensibly* he was there to teach. Latin *ostendere* (to show).

sobriquet — D: Nickname; an assumed, often humorous name; as, "a *sobriquet* both childish and basically unsuitable." French.

lugubrious — A: Mournful or sad, especially in an exaggerated way; as, "a look of *lugubrious* disapproval." Latin *lugere* (to bewail).

frisson — A: A shudder or shiver arising from fear, joy, excitement; as, "an agreeable *frisson* of terror." French.

venue — B: Meeting or gathering place. Also, location for a trial. French, from *venir* (to come).

recrimination — C: Countercharge; as, "Friendship there could deteriorate into gossip, *recriminations* and betrayal." Latin re- (again) and *criminari* (to accuse).

vicarious — D: Serving as a substitute; as, "a brief, *vicarious* immortality." Latin *vicarius*.

histrionic — D: Excessively dramatic; as, "He beat his hands against the door. It seemed a *histrionic* gesture." Latin *histrio* (actor).

derisory — C: Expressing mockery or contempt; ridiculous; as, "What you pay [in rent] is *derisory*. It doesn't even cover repairs." Latin *deridere* (to laugh).

unprepossessing — B: Unimpressive; not especially attractive; as, "a particularly *unprepossessing* face." Latin *in-* (not) and *possidere* (to possess).

condone — A: To forgive or overlook a wrongdoing; as, a man "who had never supposed that the evil of the world should be *condoned*." Latin *condonare*.

rail — C: To attack with harsh or insulting language; complain; as, "She *railed* at me like a woman possessed." Latin *ragere* (to bray).

Vocabulary Ratings

    9 — 11 correct . . . Good
    12 — 17 correct . . . Excellent
    18 — 20 correct . . . Exceptional

AND AWAY WE GO

Stalking through the cornfield . . . Blazing past the fire station . . . Slipping through the lingerie department . . . Tripping through the travel agency . . . Lumbering through the woods . . .

—DAVE AND EMILY NOSSAMAN

MUSIC TO THE EARS

The following words come from the witty musicals of Gilbert and Sullivan—The Mikado, The Pirates of Penzance, H.M.S. Pinafore and others that have delighted millions. Choose the answer you think is correct. Turn the page for your score.

mope *v.* — A: to be dejected. B: wipe away. C: rebuff. D: mumble.

oration *n.* — A: speech. B: choral sound. C: ceremony. D: decoration.

quick *n.* — A: short ribbon. B: steep path. C: anything flimsy. D: deepest feelings.

dictatorial *adj.* — A: clearly spoken. B: overbearing. C: repetitious. D: cranky.

paradox *n.* — A: parallel line. B: traditional belief. C: apparent contradiction. D: embarrassing muddle.

dissemble (dih SEM b'l) *v.* — A: to disguise. B: take apart. C: scatter. D: fluster.

malediction (mal eh DIK shun) *n.* — A: mispronunciation. B: soothing language. C: habit. D: curse.

bulwark *n.* — A: defense. B: firmness. C: compartment. D: platform.

solecism (SOL eh siz em) *n.* — A: wise saying. B: witty quip. C: clever argument. D: grammatical error.

succinct *adj.* — A: sarcastic. B: outspoken. C: terse. D: slow and careful.

❝Laughter translates into any language.**❞**

—*"Graffiti," McNaught Syndicate*

> **"**Let us read and let us dance—two amusements that will never do any harm to the world.**"**
>
> —*VOLTAIRE*

---

reprobation *n.* — A: review. B: disapproval. C: endorsement. D: aversion.

bias *n.* — A: fairness. B: logical thought. C: prejudice. D: puzzling situation.

avidity *n.* — A: mental keenness. B: bitterness. C: thoughtless haste. D: intense desire.

suppliant (SUP lee unt) *n.* — one who A: is a flatterer. B: has flexibility. C: fulfills a need. D: asks humbly.

propriety (pruh PRY eh tee) *n.* — A: truthfulness. B: punctuality. C: respectability. D: esteem.

atone *v.* — A: to sing together. B: repent. C: adjust to. D: clarify.

induce *v.* — A: to persuade. B: meet. C: accompany. D: decrease.

plaintiff *n.* — person who A: sues. B: is unhappy. C: defends. D: implores.

conundrum (kuh NUN drum) *n.* — A: joke. B: illustration. C: type of prayer. D: riddle.

unavailing *adj.* — A: restrained. B: out of touch. C: useless. D: inevitable.

> **"**The other arts persuade us, but music takes us by surprise.**"**
>
> —*EDUARD HANSLICK*

 ANSWERS

mope — A: To be dejected; gloomy; as, "I used to *mope* and sigh and pant, just like a lovesick boy." Middle Dutch *moppen* (to pout).

oration — A: Public speech, usually formal; as, "All thieves who could afford my fees relied on my *orations*." Latin *orare* (to speak).

quick — D: Deepest feelings; sensitive flesh under fingernails; as, "Your words cut me to the *quick*." Old English *cwicu* (living).

dictatorial — B: Overbearing; domineering; as, "His energetic fist should be ready to resist a *dictatorial* word." Latin *dictare* (to say often).

paradox — C: Apparent contradiction that may contain a truth; as, "We lay and sobbed upon the rocks, until to somebody occurred a startling *paradox*." Greek *paradoxos* (unbelievable).

dissemble — A: To disguise; hide one's identity; as, "Red, am I? and round — and rosy! Maybe, for I have *dissembled* well." Latin *dis-* (completely) and *simulare* (to pretend).

malediction — D: Curse; slander; as, "We'll finish his moral affliction by a very complete *malediction*." Latin *malus* (bad) and *dicere* (to speak).

bulwark — A: Defense; protection; as, "Never forget that they [sailors] are the *bulwarks* of England's greatness." Middle English *bulwerk*.

solecism — D: Grammatical error; as, "*solecisms* that society would never pardon." Greek *soloikos* (speaking incorrectly).

succinct — C: Terse; concise; as, "So, he decreed in words *succinct*, that all who flirted, leered or winked should be beheaded." Latin *succinctus*.

reprobation — B: Disapproval; scolding; as, "In uttering a *reprobation* to any British tar [sailor], I try to speak with moderation, but you have gone too far." Latin *reprobare* (to reject).

bias — C: Prejudice; inclination; as, "Free from *bias* of every kind, this trial must be tried." French *biais* (slant, slope).

avidity — D: Intense desire; greediness; as, "To dine on chops and roly-poly pudding with *avidity*." Latin *avere* (to crave).

suppliant — D: One who asks humbly; as, "Behold a *suppliant* at your feet." Latin *supplicare* (to beg).

propriety — C: Respectability; conformity; as, "*Propriety*, we know, says we ought to stay." Middle English *propriete*.

atone — B: To repent; make amends; as, "Oh, perjured lover, *atone, atone!*" Middle English *atonen* (to reconcile).

induce — A: To persuade, often subtly; as, "An official utterance might *induce* her to look upon your offer in its proper light." Latin *in-* (in) and *ducere* (to lead).

plaintiff — A: Person who sues; as, "Oh, listen to the *plaintiff's* case." Old French *plaintif* (complaining).

conundrum — D: Riddle answered by a pun; as, "Good fellow in *conundrums* you are speaking . . . . The answer to them vainly I am seeking." Origin unknown.

unavailing — C: Useless; futile; as, "I thank you for your proffered solace, but it is *unavailing*." English *un-* (not) and Latin *valere* (to be strong).

Vocabulary Ratings
> 9 — 11 correct ... Good
> 12 — 17 correct . . . Excellent
> 18 — 20 correct . . . Exceptional

MUSICAL MIGHT-HAVE-BEENS

Bach "To the Future"

Handel "With Care"

Haydn "Go Seek"

Verdi "Interesting" —James M. Garber

MAGICAL MYSTERY

"There are two types of geniuses, the 'ordinary' and the 'magicians,'" says one admirer of Richard Feynman in a biography of the late physicist, who certainly belonged to the latter category. The following words are taken from the book. Turn the page to find your score.

rebuttal *n.* — A: suggestion. B: rebuke. C: unkind refusal. D: opposing argument.

metamorphosis (met uh MOR fuh sis) *n.* — A: deep sleep. B: transformation. C: periodic recurrence. D: significant event.

caldron *n.* — A: computer term. B: kettle. C: static electricity. D: laser fusion.

esoteric (es uh TER ik) *adj.* — A: ancient. B: difficult to understand. C: wondrous. D: light and frothy.

cadre (KAD ree) *n.* — A: hidden source. B: follower. C: key group. D: student.

rigor *n.* — A: anxiety. B: strictness. C: strength. D: vitality.

tenet *n.* — A: experiment. B: mathematical equation. C: observation. D: belief or principle.

vantage *n.* — A: competitive superiority. B: pride. C: cutting edge. D: turning point.

interpolate *v.* — A: to clarify. B: investigate. C: reverse. D: insert.

superlative *adj.* — A: supreme. B: powerful. C: legendary. D: necessary.

❝We all live under the same sky, but we don't all have the same horizon.**❞**

—Konrad Adenauer

"Some things have to be believed to be seen."

—RALPH HODGSON

---

rectify *v.* — A: to break. B: correct. C: build. D: criticize.

truism *n.* — A: guess. B: questionable statement. C: discovery.
D: obvious truth.

bailiwick *n.* — A: area of authority. B: woven container.
C: false lead. D: complicated formula.

gestation *n.* — A: pregnancy. B: bodily motion. C: spurt of activity.
D: period of quiet.

innate *adj.* — A: resourceful. B: inborn. C: foolish. D: spontaneous.

subordinate (suh BOR dih nate) *v.* — A: to guide craftily.
B: hand over. C: put under authority. D: add to.

embody *v.* — A: to make similar. B: incorporate. C: separate.
D: solidify.

connive *v.* — A: to conspire. B: provoke. C: blame. D: tease.

primer (PRIM er) *n.* — A: chemical symbol. B: introductory textbook. C: principal force. D: primitive drive.

teleological (teel ee ah LODGE ih k'l) *adj.* — related to the study of
A: ultimate purposes. B: analytical procedures. C: communication. D: historic events.

**"Never a daisy grows but a mystery guides the
growing."**

—RICHARD REALF

 ANSWERS

rebuttal — D: An opposing argument; as, "He offered the mildest of the many possible *rebuttals*." Old French *rebuter* (to thrust back, push).

metamorphosis — B: Transformation; complete change; as, the *metamorphosis* of a caterpillar into a butterfly. Greek *meta-morphoun* (to transform).

caldron — B: Large kettle; also, an agitated condition; as, "the famous *caldron* of physicist Ernest Lawrence's laboratory." Latin *calidus* (warm).

esoteric — B: Difficult to understand; as, "Younger scientists explored *esoteric* new domains." Greek *esoteros* (inner).

cadre — C: Key group; nucleus of trained people; as, "He left behind a small *cadre* of students." Latin *quadrum* (square).

rigor — B: Strictness or severity in judgment or conduct; as, His childhood was a "combination of freedom and moral *rigor*." Latin *rigere* (to be stiff).

tenet — D: Belief or principle; as, "Only rarely did they express [their creed's] *tenets*, but they lived by them." Latin *tenere* (to hold).

vantage — A: Competitive superiority; position giving a broad perspective; as, the *vantage* that comes from experience. Old French *avantage*.

interpolate — D: To insert new material that may distort a text; mathematically, to estimate a missing value. Latin *interpo-lare* (to polish, corrupt).

superlative — A: Supreme; of outstanding quality. Latin *superlatus* (exaggerated).

rectify — B: To correct; adjust; amend; as, "to *rectify* his mother's checkbook." Latin *rectificare*.

truism — D: Obvious, self-evident truth; as, "It became an instant *truism* that science meant power." Old English *treowth* (truth).

bailiwick — A: Area of authority, interest or skill; as, Quantum mechanics was his *bailiwick*. English *bailiff* (deputy sheriff) and *wick* (village).

gestation — A: Pregnancy. Also, the conception and development of an idea; as, the *gestation* of a new theory. Latin *gerere* (to bear).

innate — B: Inborn; existing naturally, rather than acquired; as, "Children are *innate* scientists." Latin *innasci*.

subordinate — C: To put under the authority of another; as, "Some [scientists] *subordinated* their own abilities to his." Latin *subordinare*.

embody — B: To incorporate; represent; give form to; as, "Most physicists were now persuaded that the atom *embodied* . . . electrons, protons and neutrons." Prefix *em-* (in) and *body*.

connive — A: To conspire; cooperate secretly; as, They *connived* to alert President Roosevelt to the possibility of an atom bomb. Latin *connivere* (to close the eyes, wink).

primer — B: Introductory textbook covering the basic elements of a subject; as, a *primer* on mathematical methods. Latin *primus* (first).

teleological — A: Related to the study of ultimate purposes in natural phenomena; as, The *teleological* question, what is the meaning of life? Greek *telos* (end) and *-logy* (study of).

Vocabulary Ratings

     9 — 11 correct . . . Good

     12 — 17 correct . . . Excellent

     18 — 20 correct . . . Exceptional

❝Everyone is a genius at least once a year.**❞**

—G. C. Lichtenberg

There's music in words, especially in the cadences of poetry, from which the verbs in this list come. Indicate your answer, then turn the page to rate your score.

vegetate — A: to be passive. B: be health conscious. C: eat no meat. D: rest.

sedate — A: to calm. B: give up. C: sit. D: keep under control.

stipulate — A: to undertake. B: be firm. C: specify. D: fasten tightly.

acclimate (AK luh mate) — A: to moderate. B: acquire. C: reach a climax. D: adapt to.

berate — A: to underestimate. B: scold. C: make the cry of a donkey. D: classify.

relegate — A: to control by rules. B: act as a spokesman. C: put off or delay. D: send away.

equivocate — A: to stir up. B: be evasive. C: balance out. D: see all sides of a question.

renovate — A: to change. B: restore. C: replace. D: examine.

precipitate — A: to cause to happen. B: leap. C: clarify. D: make public.

exonerate (ig ZAHN uh rate) — A: to become larger. B: free from blame. C: compliment excessively. D: destroy utterly.

innovate — A: to give courage to. B: study the cosmos. C: re-establish. D: introduce something new.

WORD FOR WORD

Words are the clothes that thoughts wear.

—*Ronald Geller*

Metaphors are ideas sporting borrowed coats.

—*Emily Stronk*

Poetry is prose dressed in Sunday best.

—*O. C. M.*

extrapolate (ik STRAP uh late) — A: to firm up. B: estimate.
C: remove from. D: add to.

satiate (SAY she ate) — A: to desire. B: be cruel. C: use ridicule.
D: glut.

recapitulate — A: to surrender. B: be indecisive. C: summarize.
D: retract.

undulate — A: to quiver and quake. B: move in waves.
C: revolve around. D: become seasick.

gesticulate (jeh STIK yoo late) — A: to frown. B: develop slowly.
C: make expressive gestures. D: pronounce distinctly.

immolate — A: to offer in sacrifice. B: keep from moving.
C: immerse completely. D: shield from.

militate — A: to challenge. B: lay down the law. C: arbitrate.
D: influence against.

crenelate (KREN uh late) — A: to wrinkle. B: notch.
C: decorate with ribbons. D: do brain studies.

perpetuate — A: to cause to continue. B: sulk. C: impose.
D: bring about.

66In the end, the poem is not a thing we see; it is,
rather, a light by which we may see—and what
we see is life. **99**

—*ROBERT PENN WARREN*

vegetate — A: To live a life of passivity, monotony or mental inactivity; also, to grow as a plant. Latin *vegetare* (to quicken, enliven).

sedate — A: To calm or quiet by administering a drug; as, to *sedate* a ferocious animal in a zoo. Latin *sedare* (to settle).

stipulate — C: To specify as an essential condition of an agreement; as, He *stipulated* that the software program must be easy to learn. Latin *stipulari* (to bargain).

acclimate — D: To adapt to new conditions or circumstances; as, to *acclimate* to the slower pace of the tropics. French *acclimater*.

berate — B: To give a prolonged, severe and sometimes abusive scolding. English prefix *be-* (thoroughly) and *rate* (to chide).

relegate — D: To send away, especially to a less desirable situation; as, to *relegate* a Major League baseball player to the minors. Also, to delegate; as, to *relegate* a problem to a committee. Latin *relegare*.

equivocate — B: To be evasive, vague or ambiguous so as to mislead or conceal; hedge. Latin *aequus* (equal) and *vocare* (to call).

renovate — B: To restore to a good condition; as, The family *renovated* an old house. Latin *renovare*.

precipitate — A: To cause to happen suddenly; bring on; as, His unfortunate remark *precipitated* a bitter argument. Latin *praecipitare* (to hurl downward).

exonerate — B: To free or clear from blame; absolve; as, to *exonerate* an accused person on the basis of fresh evidence. Latin *ex-* (out) and *onus* (burden).

innovate — D: To introduce something new or create a novel method of doing something. Latin *in-* (in) and *novare* (to make new).

extrapolate — B: To estimate; also, to draw a conclusion about something unknown based on its relevance to known facts; as, to *extrapolate* a theory about a tenth planet. Latin *extra-* (beyond) and *polire* (to polish).

satiate — D: To glut; have more than enough of anything to the point of losing interest; as, to *satiate* oneself with cheesecake. Latin *satiare* (to satisfy, fill).

recapitulate — C: To summarize concisely, as at the end of a speech or meeting; review briefly. Latin *recapitulare*.

undulate — B: To move in a smooth, wavelike or sinuous motion; as, fields of wheat *undulating* in the soft wind. Latin *unda* (wave).

gesticulate — C: To make expressive gestures with the hands and arms to add emphasis to one's words. Latin *gesticulari*.

immolate — A: To offer in sacrifice; to kill as by fire; as, The Buddhist monk, opposing the government, *immolated* himself in a bonfire. Latin *immolare* (originally, to sprinkle with sacrificial meal).

militate — D: To have a substantial influence or effect, usually against; as, The policy will *militate* against age discrimination. Latin *militare* (to serve as a soldier).

crenelate — B: To form square notches in molding; make squared-off battlements in a fortress. Old French *crénel* (notch).

perpetuate — A: To cause to continue or be remembered; as, to *perpetuate* a tradition. Latin *perpetuare*.

Vocabulary Ratings
> 9 — 11 correct . . . Good
> 12 — 17 correct . . . Excellent
> 18 — 20 correct . . . Exceptional

---

66 It's a little bit the fiddle, but lots more who holds the bow. **99**
—*WILBURN WILSON*

AN AMERICAN ORIGINAL

Mark Twain, besides being a beloved American writer, was also an inventor, a Mississippi River pilot, a humorist and a lecturer. How many of the following words, all taken from his books, do you know? Turn the page to find out.

insipid *adj.* — A: not interesting. B: slow-moving. C: lacking in thoroughness. D: easygoing.

sovereign (SOV uh rin, SOV rin) *n.* — A: entirety. B: wealth. C: ruler. D: grandeur.

singularly *adv.* — A: simply. B: extraordinarily. C: representatively. D: pointedly.

inundation *n.* — A: a sinking. B: repetition. C: flood. D: curve.

husband *v.* — A: to conserve. B: boss around. C: be fond of. D: relieve.

rude *adj.* — A: projecting. B: natural. C: everyday. D: primitive.

trammels *n.* — A: problems. B: blows or punches. C: narrow planks. D: restraints.

yaw *v.* — A: to open wide. B: change direction. C: tell tall tales. D: scold.

unfettered *adj.* — A: slim. B: without principle. C: liberated. D: careless.

somnambulist (sahm NAM byoo list) *n.* — A: magician. B: sleepwalker. C: acrobat. D: wine steward.

❝Whenever you find yourself on the side of the majority, it is time to pause and reflect.**❞**

—MARK TWAIN

IDIOMS

She's nuttier than a squirrel's breakfast. —Paul Dickson

He's as broke as the Ten Commandments.

—Quoted by Stuart Turner

---

sound *v.* — A: to leave suddenly. B: proceed. C: play the fool.
　　D: measure water depth.

remonstrate (rih MAHN strate) *v.* — A: to feel regret. B: be angry.
　　C: argue in protest. D: have sympathy for.

farce *n.* — A: social blunder. B: absurd sham. C: disorder.
　　D: falsehood.

pretext *n.* — A: false reason. B: first draft. C: introduction.
　　D: summary.

lagniappe (lan YAP) *n.* — A: compliment. B: lasso. C: mugginess.
　　D: small gift.

hobnob *v.* — A: to scold. B: flirt. C: associate with. D: snub.

finite *adj.* — A: complete. B: limited. C: exact. D: everlasting.

bogus *adj.* — A: inferior. B: spooky. C: not genuine. D: extra.

elision (ih LIZH un) *n.* — A: home of the gods. B: injury or wound.
　　C: omission of a syllable. D: careful explanation.

misnomer (mis NO mur) *n.* — A: wrong name. B: sales pitch.
　　C: random list. D: gross insult.

66There ain't no surer way to find out whether you like
people or hate them than to travel with them.**99**

—MARK TWAIN

 *ANSWERS*

insipid — A: Not interesting; without flavor; as, "the *insipid* diversion they call croquet." Latin *in-* (not) and *sapidus* (savory).

sovereign — C: Ruler; monarch; king; supreme authority. Old French *souverain*.

singularly — B: Extraordinarily; exceptionally; as, "So *singularly* clear was the water, the boat seemed to be floating in air." Latin *singularis* (single).

inundation — C: Flood; overwhelming flow; as, "A Mississippi River *inundation* is the next most wasting infliction to a fire." Latin *inundare* (to overflow).

husband — A: To conserve; use economically; make the most of. Old English *husbonda* (master of the house).

rude — D: Primitive; crude; roughly made; as, "They found some *rude* and fantastic Indian paintings." Latin *rudis*.

trammels — D: Restraints; whatever hinders free action; as, "The watchman threw off all *trammels* of date and locality." Middle English *tramaile* (fishing net).

yaw — B: To change direction in a boat or ship; swerve from side to side; as, "I *yawed* too far from shore." Origin uncertain.

unfettered — C: Liberated; free from restriction; as, "A river pilot was the only *unfettered* and entirely independent human being." English *un* (not) and Old English *feter* (chain or shackle).

somnambulist — B: Sleepwalker; as, He was a *somnambulist* who once steered a difficult passage in his sleep. Latin *somnus* (sleep) and *ambulare* (to walk).

sound — D: To measure the depth of water with a weighted line; as, The words "mark twain" mean the bottom has been *sounded* at two fathoms (12 feet). Latin *subundare* (to submerge).

remonstrate — C: To argue in protest; as, "I *remonstrated* with him about [whistling at the funeral]." Latin *remonstrare* (to demonstrate).

farce — B: Absurd sham; as, "those sorrowful *farces* we call a jury trial." Latin *farcire* (to stuff).

pretext — A: False reason to cover up the real one; excuse; as, looking for a *pretext* to find fault. Latin *praetexere* (to pretend).

lagniappe — D: Small gift, especially to a customer; as, "We picked up a word worth traveling to New Orleans to get; a nice, limber, expressive, handy word — *lagniappe*." Creole, from American Spanish *lañapa*.

hobnob — C: To associate with; as, "to *hobnob* with nobility." Originally a reference to drinking together. From Old English *habben* (to have) and *nabban* (not to have).

finite — B: Limited; having boundaries; as, a *finite* number of hours in a day. Latin *finire* (to finish).

bogus — C: Not genuine; counterfeit; as, "Nobody had ever received his *bogus* history as gospel before." Origin uncertain.

elision — C: Omission of a syllable, such as "o'er" for "over"; as, "I found the half-forgotten Southern *elisions* pleasing to my ear." Latin *elidere* (to strike out).

misnomer — A: Wrong or unsuitable name; as, " 'The Grand Holy Land Pleasure Excursion' was a *misnomer*." Old French *mesnommer* (to misname).

Vocabulary Ratings
> **9 — 11 correct . . . Good**
> **12 — 17 correct . . . Excellent**
> **18 — 20 correct . . . Exceptional**

SNIDELINERS

She's so aggravating, she'd give an aspirin a headache.

—Frank Hughes

He'd toss a drowning man both ends of a rope. —Michael R. Luna

He's so snobbish, he won't even ride in the same car as his chauffeur. —David Frost

CRITICAL JUDGMENTS

Thumbs-up ratings by reviewers can often determine the success of a TV program, book, recording or movie. What are your "critic's choice" definitions of the following words picked from reviews of the arts? Turn the page for your score.

blathering *adj.* — A: foolish-talking. B: crying. C: gossiping. D: outrageous.

buoyant *adj.* — A: shallow. B: amusing. C: lighthearted. D: brisk.

static *adj.* — A: muddled. B: bunched-up. C: tedious. D: stationary.

rue *v.* — A: to scold. B: be unsympathetic. C: designate. D: regret.

evocative *adj.* — A: challenging. B: stimulating memories. C: loud. D: speaking clearly.

gull *v.* — A: to soothe. B: soar. C: deceive. D: irritate.

execrable (EK sih kruh b'l) *adj.* — A: detestable. B: harsh. C: flawless. D: extraordinary.

muse *v.* — A: to fuss over. B: mumble. C: yearn deeply. D: ponder.

brio (BREE oh) *n.* — A: danger. B: vivacity. C: informality. D: sluggishness.

deracinate (dih RAS uh nate) *v.* — A: to distribute. B: explain carefully. C: solve logically. D: uproot.

imprecation *n.* — A: belief. B: warning. C: curse. D: blessing.

SO AND SO'S

He's so crooked he could hide behind a corkscrew. —Lane Kirkland

He's so tough he looks as if he flosses with piano wire.
—Christopher Buckley

Coffee so strong it would keep you up three days after you died. —Marv Albert

He's so honest you could play checkers with him over the phone. —H. Jackson Brown, Jr.

---

pedestrian *adj.* — A: long-term. B: dull. C: healthy. D: dependable.

trilogy (TRILL uh jee) *n.* — A: set of three. B: musical scale. C: medical priority. D: long story.

specious (SPEE shus) *adj.* — A: genuine. B: roomy. C: misleading. D: dreamy.

contrive *v.* — A: to strive after. B: work together. C: think up. D: tempt.

cameo *n.* — A: minor role for actor. B: something added. C: old-fashioned plot. D: style or manner.

audacious *adj.* — A: conceited. B: loud. C: full of energy. D: recklessly bold.

sycophantic (sik uh FAN tik) *adj.* — A: cowardly. B: flattering. C: highly intelligent. D: rhythmic.

prolific *adj.* — A: skillful. B: wordy. C: productive. D: proud.

stilted *adj.* — A: stiff. B: forceful. C: carefully worked out. D: repressed.

PAN ALLEY
From a review: "Television is so dull this season that children are doing their homework."
—PEMBROKE, MASS., *SILVER LAKE NEWS*

Comment on a show touted as light and breezy: "I was expecting fluff, but this was lint."
—CAROLYN FORD

 *ANSWERS*

blathering — A: Talking in a foolish way and usually at length; as, These characters are *blathering* idiots. Old Norse *blathr* (nonsense).

buoyant — C: Showing a light-hearted resilience of spirit; as, She bubbles with *buoyant* energy. Also, able to float. Perhaps Spanish *boyar* (to float).

static — D: Stationary; not moving; inactive; as, The actor's performance was *static* and lifeless. Greek *statikos* (causing to stand).

rue — D: To regret a mistake; feel remorse or repentance; as, He *rued* his decision to direct the controversial film. Old English *hreowan* (to regret).

evocative — B: Stimulating a memory, mood or mental image; as, The country-western singer's ballads are magically *evocative*. Latin *evocare* (to call out).

gull — C: To deceive or cheat; as, She was *gulled* into going off with the con man. Origin uncertain.

execrable — A: Detestable; abominable; very bad; as, He writes *execrable* fiction. Latin *exsecrari* (to curse).

muse — D: To ponder; consider thoughtfully; meditate; as, "It's more than an action story," the reviewer *mused*. Old French *muser*.

brio — B: Vivacity; liveliness; dash and spirit; as, The play has a lot of *brio* and a few bumps. Italian, from Celtic *brigos*.

deracinate — D: To uproot; eradicate; remove from a natural environment; as, to describe the pain of being *deracinated* from one's native land. French *de-* (out) and *racine* (root).

imprecation — C: Vengeful curse or wish that calls for a calamity to fall on someone; as, a man of muttered *imprecations* and brooding silences. Latin *imprecari* (to invoke evil on).

pedestrian — B: Dull and ordinary; without vitality, imagination or distinction; as, a *pedestrian* film. Latin *pedester* (on foot).

trilogy — A: Set of three related works; as, the second novel of the *trilogy*. Greek *tri-* (three) and *logos* (word).

specious — C: Misleading; seeming to be true but actually false; as, The rumor raised its *specious* head again. Latin *speciosus* (beautiful, plausible).

contrive — C: To think up; plan cleverly; conspire; as, The scenes were the most bizarre that the director could *contrive*. Old French *controver*.

cameo — A: Minor role for an actor, especially a famous one; short piece of descriptive writing. Primary meaning is engraved gem Italian *cammeo*.

audacious — D: Recklessly bold; highly original and inventive; uninhibited; as, The director's imagery has always been *audacious*. Latin *audere* (to dare).

sycophantic — B: Flattering in a self-seeking, servile way; as, The movie star's biography is a glossy, *sycophantic* portrait. Greek *sykophantes* (informer).

prolific — C: Highly productive; turning out many creative works; fertile; as, She is a *prolific* writer. Latin *proles* (offspring).

stilted — A: Stiff; artificially formal; pompous; without a sense of grace and flow; as, a play with *stilted* situations and dialogue.

Vocabulary Ratings
    9 — 11 correct . . . Good
    12 — 17 correct . . . Excellent
    18 — 20 correct . . . Exceptional

VOCAL CHORDS
He had a voice so husky
it could pull a dog sled.

—RAYMOND TILLMANN

KEYS TO LEARNING

Keeping your spoken and written language fresh takes constant effort, learning new words day by day. In this quiz, choose the word or phrase that best defines the key word. Turn the page to check your score. Try to add any missed words to your permanent collection.

tender *v.* — A: to offer. B: sympathize. C: hesitate. D: suggest.

ardor *n.* — A: persuasion. B: warmth of emotion.
C: deep conviction. D: musical inclination.

clinical *adj.* — A: abstract. B: cosmetic. C: directly observed.
D: drug-induced.

sufferance *n.* — A: right to vote. B: inner peace.
C: give-and-take situation. D: patient endurance.

boisterous *adj.* — A: humorously pompous. B: carefree and
nonchalant. C: noisy and cheerful. D: invigorating.

factoid *n.* — A: splinter group. B: obvious mistake. C: unverified
information. D: synthetic object.

beggar *v.* — A: to explain. B: make seem inadequate.
C: attempt to deceive. D: impose limitations.

conversant *adj.* — A: talkative. B: courteous. C: well-informed.
D: creative.

icon *n.* — A: symbol. B: false representation. C: document.
D: destroyer of images.

obstinate *adj.* — A: protruding. B: unyielding. C: foolish.
D: self-assertive.

❝You will stay young as long as you learn, form new
habits and don't mind being contradicted.**❞**

—MARIE VON EBNER-ESCHENBACH

> **"**To profit from good advice requires more wisdom than to give it.**"**
>
> —JOHN CHURTON COLLINS

---

spontaneous *adj.* — A: well-timed. B: comical. C: explosive.
D: unplanned.

fraught (FRAWT) *adj.* — A: full of. B: manufactured. C: empty.
D: bitter.

cashier *v.* — A: to assist. B: save. C: win. D: dismiss.

prophetic *adj.* — A: scolding. B: predictive. C: obscure. D: ancient.

sundry *adj.* — A: countless. B: changing. C: various.
D: disconnected.

implication *n.* — something A: proven. B: cursed. C: causing doubt.
D: hinted at.

endeavor *v.* — A: to look over. B: please. C: attempt.
D: bring about.

impoverished *adj.* — A: imposed upon. B: severely penalized.
C: made poor. D: heavily burdened.

pithiness *n.* — A: ridicule. B: indecency. C: conciseness.
D: determination.

tremulous *adj.* — A: delicate. B: tranquil. C: inadequate.
D: quivering.

> **"**What I admire in Columbus is not his having discovered a world but his having gone to search for it on the faith of an opinion.**"**
>
> —A. ROBERT TURGOT

 *ANSWERS*

tender — A: To offer or present anything for acceptance or approval; as, The administration expected the official to *tender* his resignation. Latin *tendere* (to extend).

ardor — B: Intense warmth of emotion; zeal; as, The governor spoke with *ardor* of the need to improve the educational system. Latin *ardor* (flame).

clinical — C: Relating to the direct observation and treatment of patients; as, *Clinical* tests showed him to be in good health. Greek *klinikos* (of the bed).

sufferance — D: Patient endurance; capacity to tolerate pain or distress; as, She bore the harsh winters with stoic *sufferance*. Latin *sufferre* (to undergo).

boisterous — C: Noisy and cheerful; rowdy and unrestrained; as, The grandfather gave a *boisterous* laugh. Middle English *boistreous* (crude).

factoid — C: Unverified or fictitious information presented as fact; as, a report filled with *factoids*. Also, obscure, trivial information. From *fact* and Greek *-oid* (resembling).

beggar — B: To make descriptions or comparisons seem inadequate or useless; outdo; as, a spectacular scene that *beggars* description. Middle English (to make poor).

conversant — C: Well-informed; familiar with; as, a sales manager *conversant* with a competitor's marketing plan. Latin *conversari* (to keep company with).

icon — A: Symbol; image; representation; as, Unfortunately, sometimes a mansion becomes the main *icon* of worldly success. Greek *eikon* (image).

obstinate — B: Unyielding; unreasonably resolved to have one's way; stubborn; as, We call someone "persevering" in a good cause and *"obstinate"* in a bad one. Latin *obstinare* (to persist).

spontaneous — D: Unplanned; coming naturally and freely on its own; as, the audience's *spontaneous* applause. Latin *sponte* (of its own accord).

fraught — A: Full of; involving; laden; as, The government's plan was *fraught* with difficulties. Middle Dutch *vrachten* (to load a ship).

cashier — D: To dismiss from a position of authority or trust, especially in disgrace; as, The lieutenant was *cashiered* from his regiment. Old French *casser* (to annul).

prophetic — B: Predictive, often ominously so; foreshadowing. Greek *prophetikos*.

sundry — C: Various; miscellaneous; as, *sundry* household tasks. Old English *syndrig* (separate).

implication — D: Something hinted at but not expressed in overt terms; as, the *implication* that the bookkeeper was involved in the fraud. Latin *implicare* (to enfold).

endeavor — C: To make an attempt; strive; as, The United Nations *endeavors* to bring peace to the region. Old French *deveir* (duty).

impoverished — C: Made poor; as, an *impoverished* nation. Also, without strength or richness; as, an *impoverished* vocabulary. From *in* and Latin *pauper* (poor).

pithiness — C: Conciseness; fullness of meaning with brevity of expression; as, The minister had the gift of *pithiness*. Old English *pith* (kernel, pit of a fruit).

tremulous — D: Quivering from nervousness, grief, weakness or fear; as, The survivor spoke in a *tremulous* voice. Latin *tremere* (to tremble).

Vocabulary Ratings

    9 — 11 correct . . . Good
    12 — 17 correct . . . Excellent
    18 — 20 correct . . . Exceptional

LIVING DREAMS

These challenging words come from Langston Hughes, a man who led a story-book life. He was a sailor, janitor, song-writer and teacher, as well as an author and poet who won wide recognition for his work. How many of these words from his book The Big Sea *do you know? Turn the page to find your score.*

contempt *n.* — A: skepticism. B: anger. C: judgment. D: scorn.

melodramatic *adj.* — A: musical. B: evil. C: comic.
D: overly theatrical.

renaissance (REN uh sahns) *n.* — A: new information. B: fluency of expression. C: deterioration. D: rebirth.

innuendo *n.* — A: secrecy. B: unpleasant insinuation. C: funny remark. D: quiet explanation.

meager *adj.* — A: shoddy. B: superficial. C: inadequate. D: willful.

vespers *n.* — A: dizziness. B: evening prayer. C: form of poetry.
D: chorale.

dire *adj.* — A: narrow. B: enraged. C: dreadful. D: meaningful.

personage *n.* — one who is A: inconspicuous. B: religious.
C: sophisticated. D: important.

scintillating (SIN tuh layt ing) *adj.* — A: bitterly sarcastic.
B: brilliantly clever. C: fragile. D: unpredictable.

pretension *n.* — A: insolent behavior. B: insupportable claim.
C: undisputed right. D: extreme selfishness.

rollicking *adj.* — A: upsetting. B: pensive. C: lighthearted.
D: mischievous.

PORTRAIT GALLERY

It wasn't that he remembered; it was that he never forgot.

—James Grady

> **❝**Humor is laughing at what you haven't got when you ought to have it.**❞**
>
> —Langston Hughes

---

dialect *n.* — A: local language. B: interrogation. C: conversation. D: systematic reasoning.

solicitude *n.* — A: concern. B: peacefulness. C: seclusion. D: request.

amulet *n.* — A: small ambulance. B: charm. C: jewel. D: bottle.

patronage *n.* — A: collaboration. B: entitlement program. C: sponsorship. D: disadvantage.

grandiloquent *adj.* — A: spacious. B: light. C: glamorous. D: pompous.

millennium *n.* — A: suffering. B: period of joy. C: great flood. D: eternity.

literati (lit uh RAH tee) *n.* — A: intellectuals. B: those who put on airs. C: pampered group. D: the literal-minded.

impromptu *adj.* — A: rigid. B: uninhibited. C: improvised. D: changeable.

concoct *v.* — A: to make a show of. B: outline. C: invent. D: deceive.

> **❝**We must teach our children to dream with their eyes open.**❞**
>
> —Harry Edwards, quoted by Dennis Wyss in Time

ANSWERS

contempt — D: Scorn; disdain; as, "My father had *contempt* for all poor people." Latin *contemptus*.

melodramatic — D: Overly theatrical; highly emotional; as, his *melodramatic* act of throwing all his books into the sea. Greek *melos* (song) and *drama*.

renaissance — D: Rebirth in the arts and learning; as, "The 1920s were the years of Manhattan's black *Renaissance*." Latin *re-* (again) and *nascere* (to be born).

innuendo — B: Unpleasant insinuation; as, "The two would fling big words about with swift and punning *innuendo*." Latin, from *innuere* (to nod; hint).

meager — C: Inadequate; scanty; as, "a *meager* diet of beef and beans." Latin *macer*.

vespers — B: Church service held in the evening; evensong; as, "The three aging Mexican sisters always invited me to *vespers*." Middle English (evening star).

dire — C: Dreadful; ominous; urgent; as, "a wonderful rhythmical sermon, all moans and shouts and cries and *dire* pictures of hell." Latin *dirus* (fearful).

personage — D: Important or distinguished person; as, "Some royal *personage* arrived, a Scandinavian prince . . ." Latin *persona* (actor's mask).

scintillating — B: Brilliantly clever; witty; sparkling; as, *scintillating* conversation. Latin *scintillare*.

pretension — B: Insupportable or unfounded claim to a right or distinction; as, "She had great scorn for all *pretensions*, academic or otherwise." Latin praetendere (to pretend).

rollicking — C: Lighthearted; full of high spirits; as, "*Shuffle Along* was a honey of a show; swift, funny, *rollicking*." Perhaps a blend of English *roll* and *frolic*.

dialect — A: Local language or speech of a particular group; as, He tried to reproduce their *dialect* in his writing. Greek *dia-* (between) and *legein* (to talk).

solicitude — A: Deep concern; thoughtful attention; as, "It was too late in the evening for such *solicitude*." Latin *sollicitudo*.

amulet — B: A charm; object worn to keep off bad luck, harm and the like; as, "They gave me a little *amulet* of the Virgin of Guadalupe." Latin *amuletum*.

patronage — C: Sponsorship; clientele; political favors; as, Without black *patronage*, the small clubs in Harlem failed. Latin *patronus* (benefactor).

grandiloquent — D: Pompous in speaking; as, "He never talks *grandiloquently* about democracy or Americanism — he lives them with sincerity." Latin *grandis* (great) and *loqui* (to speak).

millennium — B: Period of joy, peace and prosperity; as, "Some Harlemites thought the *millennium* had come." Latin *mille* (thousand) and *annus* (year).

literati — A: Intellectuals; literary or scholarly people; as, "He returned to Harlem to impart his precepts to the *literati.*" Latin.

impromptu — C: Improvised; spur of the moment; as, *impromptu* entertaining. Latin.

concoct — C: To invent; make up; contrive; as, "his fabulously *concocted* stories." Latin *concoquere* (to boil together).

Vocabulary Ratings
    9 — 11 correct . . . Good
    12 — 17 correct . . . Excellent
    18 — 20 correct . . . Exceptional

❝If only the sun-drenched celebrities are being noticed and worshiped, then our children are going to have a tough time seeing value in the shadows, where the thinkers, probers and scientists are keeping society together.**❞**

—RITA DOVE, QUOTED IN NEW YORK TIMES

TO THE SKY

The words in a well-developed vocabulary are like the sturdy rungs in a ladder that help to make life's climb easier, as well as more pleasurable and successful. Take this quiz to check your progress; then turn the page for the correct answers.

concession *n.* — A: admission. B: courtesy. C: head injury.
    D: addition.
pallor *n.* — A: paleness. B: inflammation. C: paralysis. D: stretcher.
quagmire *n.* — A: quarry. B: pitfall. C: marsh.
    D: subatomic particle.
plangent *adj.* — A: overripe. B: flat. C: loud and reverberating.
    D: robust.
demographics *n.* — A: governmental procedures. B: process of
    decoding. C: visual demonstration. D: population statistics.
vex *v.* — A: to fuss. B: annoy. C: bewitch. D: shame.
legerdemain (lej er duh MAIN) *n.* — A: sleight of hand.
    B: nonsense. C: act of postponing. D: storytelling.
palpably *adv.* — A: throbbingly. B: carefully. C: obviously.
    D: sentimentally.
course *v.* — A: to ruffle. B: plan. C: denounce. D: flow.
buttress *n.* — A: accessory. B: support. C: tower. D: busybody.
canvass *v.* — A: to spread out. B: ask for opinions. C: criticize.
    D: cover up.

"Life begins as a quest of the child for the man and ends as a journey by the man to rediscover the child.**"**

—Laurens van der Post, The Lost World of the Kalahari (Morrow)

> **"**History celebrates few persons who waited for inspiration.**"**
>
> —NED ARTHUR

---

gamy *adj.* — A: dashing. B: risky. C: plucky. D: sportsmanlike.

chapfallen *adj.* — A: angry. B: rejected. C: untidy. D: dejected.

hacienda (hah see EN duh) *n.* — A: grape arbor. B: after-meal nap.
C: ranch. D: porch.

in concert *adv.* — A: sympathetically. B: together. C: apart.
D: publicly.

moribund *adj.* — A: coming to an end. B: deferring or delaying.
C: binding securely. D: witty in a mean way.

onerous (OHN uhr us) *adj.* — A: threatening. B: immense.
C: bad-smelling. D: burdensome.

rationalize *v.* — A: to parcel out. B: explain in minute detail.
C: justify. D: be optimistic.

philippic (fih LIP ik) *n.* — A: humorous remark. B: bitter verbal
denunciation. C: wise saying. D: ironic observation.

synonymous *adj.* — A: alike. B: boring. C: unknown. D: unvarying.

NIGHT LINES
The sky pulled a dark sheet over us and pinned it with stars.
—BRYCE COURTENAY

 *ANSWERS*

concession — A: Admission, compromise, acknowledgment; as, mutual *concessions* of management and labor. Latin *concedere* (to yield).

pallor — A: Unusual paleness from ill health, fear, shock; as, the *pallor* of someone with heat stroke. Latin.

quagmire — C: Marsh; wet, soft ground; extremely difficult situation to get out of; as, a financial *quagmire*. English *quag* (bog) and *mire* (soggy ground).

plangent — C: Beating with a loud, deep, reverberating sound that rises and falls like breaking waves; as, *plangent* music for soap operas. Latin *plangere* (to beat).

demographics — D: Population statistics, such as income, purchasing habits, age; as, *Demographics* showed that the area could not support a new restaurant. Greek *demos* (people) and *graphein* (to write).

vex — B: To annoy, irritate, worry; as, to *vex* someone by being habitually late. Latin *vexare*.

legerdemain — A: Sleight of hand, as in performing magic; craftiness or trickery; as, the deft *legerdemain* of a sales pitch. French *léger de main* (light of hand).

palpably — C: Obviously; detectably; plainly; as, The actress plays a *palpably* lonely character. Latin *palpare* (to touch soothingly).

course — D: To flow or move swiftly; as, Before them *coursed* a wide river. Latin *currere* (to run).

buttress — B: Support or reinforcement; as, the stone *buttress* of a medieval cathedral, or the *buttress* of a parent's love. Old French *bouteret* (thrusting arch).

canvass — B: To ask for opinions, votes, orders; as, The reporter *canvassed* the neighborhood's residents for stories. Origin uncertain.

gamy — C: Plucky, spirited; as, a *gamy* colt. Also, slightly tainted; as, *gamy* meat. English *game*.

chapfallen — D: Dejected; downhearted; as, She was *chapfallen* at not being promoted. Literally "having the lower jaw hanging down." From English *chop* (jaw) and *fallen*.

hacienda — C: Ranch or large estate in Spain or South America. Spanish, from Latin *facienda* (things to be done or made).

in concert — B: Together; in unison, agreement or harmony; as, The Czech people acted *in concert* for political reform. Italian *concertare* (to harmonize).

moribund — A: Coming to an end; dying; outdated; as, the *moribund* policies of some nations. Latin *mori* (to die).

onerous — D: Burdensome, laborious, troublesome; as, Some writers find proofreading manuscripts an *onerous* chore. Latin *onus* (load).

rationalize — C: To justify questionable actions with plausible but untrue reasons; as, An embezzler may *rationalize* that the company doesn't need the money he steals. Latin *rationalis* (reasonable).

philippic — B: Bitter verbal denunciation or attack; as, the Colombian president's brave *philippic* against the drug cartels. Greek, from Demosthenes' speeches against King Philip of Macedon.

synonymous — A: Alike; being a synonym of; equivalent in meaning. Greek *syn-* (together) and *onyma* (name).

Vocabulary Ratings
>   9 — 11 correct . . . Good
>   12 — 17 correct . . . Excellent
>   18 — 20 correct . . . Exceptional

SKY LARKS
The clouds are playing charades.
—*JOSH CARDEN*

CATCHING WORDS

Paying attention is always important, but especially when facing the unfamiliar. Pay attention to the unfamiliar words in this quiz. Then turn the page to check your score.

garrison *n.* — A: military post. B: horse stable. C: execution by choking. D: square tower.

inadmissible *adj.* — A: unbelievable. B: false. C: unacceptable. D: inarticulate.

reprise *n.* — A: vengeance. B: repetition. C: breathing spell. D: cancellation.

deputation *n.* — A: expulsion from a country. B: delegation. C: formal argument. D: statement made under oath.

irresolute *adj.* — A: indecisive. B: careless. C: fully determined. D: scattered.

provocateur *n.* — A: agitator. B: competitor. C: negotiator. D: philosopher.

autocrat *n.* — A: member of the nobility. B: someone with absolute power. C: instructor. D: patron.

luminary *n.* — A: floodlight. B: peaceful scene. C: celebrity. D: clairvoyant person.

determinate *adj.* — A: goal-oriented. B: vague. C: crucial. D: distinct.

intuit *v.* — A: to theorize. B: suggest. C: go into a trance. D: know by hunch.

" An error doesn't become a mistake until you refuse to correct it. **"**

—O. A. BATTISTA

"God made time, but man made haste."
—IRISH PROVERB

veracity *n.* — A: speed. B: anger. C: energy. D: truthfulness.
cavalcade *n.* — A: waterfall. B: procession. C: avalanche.
   D: sumptuous banquet.
martial *adj.* — characteristic of A: war. B: marriage.
   C: a large group. D: a wetland.
encode *v.* — A: to transmit. B: pull back. C: put into cipher.
   D: intercept.
ignoble *adj.* — A: foolish. B: dishonorable. C: laughable. D: proud.
inception *n.* — A: idea. B: interruption. C: beginning.
   D: social function.
implausible *adj.* — A: inflexible. B: slipshod. C: unflappable.
   D: unlikely.
addendum *n.* — A: something added. B: calculator.
   C: order of business. D: large drum.
reticular *adj.* — A: angular. B: circular. C: bowl-shaped. D: netlike.
felicitous *adj.* — A: sentimental. B: appropriate. C: lucky.
   D: scatterbrained.

MIXED MAXIMS
Don't count your chickens before they cross the road.
Mind your own business before pleasure.
He who laughs first shall be last.
Beauty is only skin deep in the eye of the beholder.
—DIANE CROSBY IN JEFF DAVIS COUNTY, GA., LEDGER

ANSWERS

garrison — A: Military post; troops stationed in a fortified place; as, a *garrison* at the edge of the frontier. Old French *garnison.*

inadmissible — C: Unacceptable; not allowable; as, The judge ruled the evidence to be *inadmissible*. Latin *in-* (not) and *admittere* (to admit).

reprise — B: Repetition of a passage of music; as, Gershwin's *reprise* of his major theme in "An American in Paris." Old French *reprendre* (to take back).

deputation — B: Delegation; group appointed to represent others; as, The *deputation* called on a state senator. Latin *deputare* (to assign).

irresolute — A: Indecisive; hesitating; uncertain about a course of action; as, His *irresolute* nature made him a poor executive. Latin *irresolutus.*

provocateur — A: Agitator; person who provokes trouble; as, The secret police placed *provocateurs* among the dissenters. Often designated *agent provocateur*. French.

autocrat — B: Someone with unlimited power over others; as, Today few successful corporations allow an *autocrat* to preside. Greek *autokrates* (ruling by oneself).

luminary — C: Celebrity; one who enlightens or influences others; as, Many *luminaries* gathered for the all-star game. Latin *lumen* (light).

determinate — D: Distinct; having precisely defined limits; as, the *determinate* wording of a local building code. Latin *determinare* (to fix the limits of).

intuit — D: To know or learn by hunch; as, From her conversation he *intuited* a sensitive mind, serious and full of goodness. Latin *intueri* (to look at).

veracity — D: Truthfulness; honesty; accuracy; as, stories based more on humor than *veracity*. Latin *verus* (true).

cavalcade — B: Procession, especially of horseback riders or carriages; any series or sequence; as, Irving Berlin's *cavalcade* of hit songs. Latin *caballus* (horse).

martial — A: Characteristic of war or military life; as, *martial* music or a city under *martial* law. Latin, from *Mars* (Roman god of war).

encode — C: To put into cipher, a system of secret symbols. Latin *en-* (in) and *codex* (writing tablet).

ignoble — B: Dishonorable; mean-spirited; not noble in character or quality; as, So many of Stalin's *ignoble* actions stain the tapestry of history. Latin *ignobilis*.

inception — C: The beginning or start of something; as, The bride's aunt witnessed the *inception* of the couple's romance. Latin *incipere* (to begin).

implausible — D: Unlikely; difficult to believe; as, The student's elaborate excuse for being late sounded *implausible*. Latin *in-* (not) and *plaudere* (to applaud).

addendum — A: Something added; a supplement; as, The report had an *addendum* clarifying certain points. Latin *addere* (to add).

reticular — D: Netlike; intricate; tending to entangle; as, The lattice-work windows cast *reticular* shadows on the floor. Latin *reticulum* (little net).

felicitous — B: Appropriate; apt; well-suited for the occasion; as, The negotiator's *felicitous* anecdote broke the tension. Latin *felicitas* (happiness).

Vocabulary Ratings
> 9 — 11 correct . . . Good
> 12 — 17 correct . . . Excellent
> 18 — 20 correct . . . Exceptional

EVER NOTICE . . .
. . . that too many people don't know what's cooking until it boils over? —Arnold H. Glasow

PRACTICE MAKES PERFECT

Want to build up your vocabulary?
Memorize the unfamiliar words below
and use them during the next seven
days. Keep it up each week and surprise
yourself with a dramatic improvement.
Start now with the following words. Turn the page
for answers.

undergird *v.* — A: to wear away. B: give support to. C: prepare.
D: evade.

fabricate *v.* — A: to amaze. B: construct or create. C: overdecorate.
D: put on a display.

crass *adj.* — A: cruel. B: vulgar. C: shocking. D: boring.

avoirdupois (av ur duh POIZ) *n.* — A: body weight.
B: extreme caution. C: sly humor. D: indisposition.

filigree *n.* — A: beauty. B: fussiness. C: ornamental design.
D: fragile object.

shaman *n.* — A: war club. B: mythological demon. C: scam artist.
D: medicine man.

archives *n.* — A: decorative moldings. B: original models.
C: sheltered walks. D: collection of information.

treacly (TREE klee) *adj.* — A: prickly. B: pointlessly busy.
C: cloyingly sweet. D: playful.

permeate *v.* — A: to consent to. B: spread throughout. C: stabilize.
D: make permanent.

"In any contest between power and patience,

bet on patience.**"**

—W. B. PRESCOTT

Overheard at a California elementary school: "Now remember, class, if you don't learn penmanship, when you grow up you'll have to pay cash for everything."

—EDWARD T. GRANEY

---

innocuous *adj.* — A: harmless. B: simple. C: useless. D: naive.

irrefutable *adj.* — A: disreputable. B: not likely. C: original.
D: undeniable.

covert *adj.* — A: vulnerable. B: united. C: concealed. D: illegal.

nary *adj.* — A: stubborn. B: deprived. C: small-minded. D: not any.

predatory *adj.* — A: able to read minds. B: plundering. C: former.
D: easy to predict.

bravura *n.* — A: brilliance. B: conceit. C: courage. D: social ease.

remedial *adj.* — A: corrective. B: out-of-date. C: long-winded.
D: balanced.

attire *n.* — A: agenda. B: mental outlook. C: hairstyle. D: clothes.

sanctity *n.* — A: refuge. B: false piety. C: authenticity. D: holiness.

quintile (QUIN tile) *n.* — A: one-fifth. B: select group.
C: musical instrument. D: large amount.

coveted *adj.* — A: goal-oriented. B: deliberately vague.
C: intensely desired. D: promised.

Henry James, criticizing a fellow novelist: "She began several years ago writing unmitigated nonsense, and she now writes nonsense very sensibly mitigated."

 ANSWERS

undergird — B: To give support to; strengthen from the underside; provide a sound basis; as, select woods used to *undergird* ships. Combination of *under* and *gird*.

fabricate — B: To construct or create. Also, to make up; as, Art dealers conspired to *fabricate* quotations of praise. Latin *fabricari*.

crass — B: Vulgar; grossly stupid and insensitive; as, a Hollywood film, *crass* in its moralizing. Latin *crassus* (thick, dense).

avoirdupois — A: Weight of a person; as, *Avoirdupois* and strength are key factors in some sports. Old French *aveir de peis* (merchandise sold by weight).

filigree — C: Ornamental, delicate and lacelike designs, especially those made with gold or silver; as, Figure skaters trace *filigrees* in their patterns on ice. Latin *filum* (thread) and *granum* (seed).

shaman — D: Medicine man or priest in certain tribal groups who is believed to influence spirits for good or evil. Of Sanskrit origin.

archives — D: Collection of information in historical records, or place where such material is kept; as, Vast *archives* of folk medicine are being lost. Greek *archeion* (town hall).

treacly — C: Cloyingly sweet or sentimental; as, The speech was long and *treacly*. Latin *theriaca* (antidote for poison).

permeate — B: To spread throughout; pervade; affect every part of; as, Violence has *permeated* the nation's history. Latin *permeare* (to flow through).

innocuous — A: Harmless; not controversial; dull and insignificant; as, an *innocuous* plan to upgrade schools. Latin *innocuus*.

irrefutable — D: Undeniable; established beyond a doubt; certain; as, a mountain of *irrefutable* evidence. Late Latin *irrefutabilis*.

covert — C: Concealed; done secretly; disguised; as, Former *covert* aid to rebels is now directed to humanitarian projects. Old French *covrir* (to cover).

nary — D: Not; not any; as, Asked if she had regrets about her career, she answered, "*Nary* a one." Altered dialectical *ne'er a* (never a).

predatory — B: Plundering, robbing or exploiting others; as, One airline accused another of *predatory* pricing. Latin *praeda* (booty, loot).

bravura — A: Brilliance; display of boldness or daring; as, The gymnast executed her routine with *bravura*. Old Italian *bravo* (brave, bold).

remedial — A: Corrective; supplying a cure or improvement; as, *remedial* plans concerning national health care. Latin *remedium* (means of relief).

attire — D: Clothes; elegant or fine garments; as, Fashion editors keep tabs on the First Lady's *attire*. Old French *atirier* (to put in order).

sanctity — D: Holiness; quality of being sacred and inviolable; as, the *sanctity* of the lawyer-client relationship. Latin *sanctus* (holy).

quintile — A: One-fifth of a total sample; as, The *quintile* that makes up the nation's leading wage earners puts aside the most savings. Latin *quintus* (fifth).

coveted — C: Intensely desired, said especially of something belonging to another; as, a *coveted* link to the Presidential ear. Latin *cupere* (to desire).

Vocabulary Ratings
    9 — 11 correct . . . Good
    12 — 17 correct . . . Excellent
    18 — 20 correct . . . Exceptional

MODERN MAXIM

"If at first you don't succeed, deny you were even trying."

—IRV KUPCINET, CHICAGO SUN-TIMES

ONWARD AND UPWARD

Each of the following words is tougher than the one before it—until the final few, which can stump even those with the strongest vocabularies. Climb this mountain of useful words and you'll reach new vistas of understanding. Then turn the page to check your elevation.

jeopardy *n.* — A: venture. B: gamble. C: danger. D: challenge.

guerrilla *n.* — A: jungle animal. B: fighter. C: daredevil. D: cheat.

escapade *n.* — A: close call. B: surprise gift. C: long journey. D: reckless adventure.

dynasty *n.* — A: historical fiction. B: hereditary rulers. C: political junta. D: interim government.

influx *n.* — A: pulsating sound. B: removal. C: absorption. D: inflow.

euphoria *n.* — A: eccentricity. B: love. C: mystical experience. D: elation.

decor (day KOR) *n.* — A: decoration. B: manners. C: neckline. D: braid.

inertia *n.* — A: exhaustion. B: powerful force. C: sluggishness. D: stubbornness.

binary (BY nuh ree) *adj.* — made up of A: various connections. B: two parts. C: binding materials. D: unlike elements.

entente (ahn TAHNT) *n.* — A: difficulty. B: celebration. C: friendly understanding. D: secret meeting.

66Let me tell you the secret that has led me to my goal. My strength lies solely in my tenacity.**99**

—LOUIS PASTEUR

❝No one can arrive from being talented alone. God gives talent; work transforms talent into genius.**❞**
—ANNA PAVLOVA, QUOTED IN LOS ANGELES EXAMINER

---

impunity *n.* — A: exemption from penalty. B: great honesty. C: bitter criticism. D: blind self-confidence.

earthy *adj.* — A: creative. B: varied. C: uninhibited. D: heavy.

affluent *adj.* — A: important. B: agreeable. C: rich. D: poised.

omnipotent *adj.* — A: all-powerful. B: widespread. C: haughty. D: one-sided.

incursion *n.* — A: interruption. B: raid. C: insult. D: obstacle.

guileless *adj.* — A: wishy-washy. B: modest. C: straightforward. D: easygoing.

panacea (pan uh SEE uh) *n.* — A: turmoil. B: overall view. C: cure-all. D: source of problems.

empirical *adj.* — A: arrogant and demanding. B: based on experience. C: having delusions of grandeur. D: theoretical.

surname *n.* — A: assumed name. B: double name. C: family name. D: first name.

gnomic (NO mik) *adj.* — A: puzzling. B: shrunken. C: very humorous. D: wise and pithy.

❝A life of ease is a difficult pursuit.**❞**

—WILLIAM COWPER

 ANSWERS

jeopardy — C: Danger; risk of loss; peril; as, Accused of falsifying his research data, the scientist found his reputation in *jeopardy*. Old French *jeu parti* (divided game with even chances).

guerrilla — B: Fighter, especially an irregular soldier who uses hit-and-run tactics. Spanish (little war).

escapade — D: Reckless adventure or prank; as, a Halloween *escapade*. Spanish *escapar* (to escape, flee).

dynasty — B: Hereditary line of rulers; series of family members noted for wealth or success; as, the Rockefeller *dynasty*. Greek *dynasthai* (to have power).

influx — D: Inflow; inpouring; as, Mexico's *influx* of tourists. Latin *influere*.

euphoria — D: Elation; sense of well-being. Greek *eu-* (well) and *pherein* (to bear).

decor — A: Decoration; style of furnishings, colors and the like in a home or an office. French, from Latin *decor* (beauty).

inertia — C: Sluggishness; slowness to take action; as, a nation paralyzed by *inertia*. Latin, from *iners* (inactive).

binary — B: Made up of two parts: as, The analog computer is based on a *binary* system of the digits 0 and 1. Latin *bini* (two by two).

entente — C: Friendly understanding between two, or among several, nations; as, U.S.–Canadian *entente* concerning their unfortified boundary. French, from *entendre* (to understand).

impunity — A: Exemption from penalty or harmful consequences; as, He lied with *impunity*. Latin *in-* (without) and *poena* (punishment).

earthy — C: Uninhibited; natural; hearty; as, The public loved her *earthy* humor. Also, coarse, vulgar. Old English *eorthe* (earth).

affluent — C: Rich; prosperous; as, Japan has become an *affluent* society. Latin *affluere* (to flow to).

omnipotent — A: All-powerful; as, He suffered from the delusion that he was *omnipotent*. Latin *omnis* (all) and *potens* (able).

incursion — B: Sudden raid or invasion into another's territory; as, a terrorist *incursion* into Israel. Latin *incurrere* (to attack).

guileless — C: Straightforward; sincere; as, a *guileless* child. From English *guile* (slyness, cunning) and *-less* (without).

panacea — C: Cure-all for diseases or problems; as, There is no *panacea* for the world's economic ills. Greek *pan-* (all) and *akos* (healing).

empirical — B: Based on experience and observation rather than on theory; as, The *empirical* evidence was overwhelming. Greek *en-* (in) and *peira* (trial).

surname — C: Family name; the last name; as, Washington is the *surname* and George the given name of our first President. French *sur* (over) and *nom* (name).

gnomic — D: Wise and pithy; as, The preacher was famous for his *gnomic* statements. Greek *gnome* (thought, judgment).

Vocabulary Ratings
    9 — 11 correct . . . Good
    12 — 17 correct . . . Excellent
    18 — 20 correct . . . Exceptional

❝Even a sheet of paper is lighter when two people lift it.**❞**

—KOREAN PROVERB

TEXT CREDITS

This page constitutes a continuation of the copyright page at the front of the book.